UNRAVELLING SUSSEX

AROUND THE COUNTY IN RIDDLES

TONY WARD

ILLUSTRATED BY GRACE OSBORNE

The History Press

> ## 'TO INFORM, EDUCATE AND ENTERTAIN'
>
> ### were Lord Reith's founding principles for the BBC.
>
> (This is the answer to the question on the back cover.)

First published 2016

The History Press
The Mill, Brimscombe Port
Stroud, Gloucestershire, GL5 2QG
www.thehistorypress.co.uk

© Tony Ward, 2016
Illustrations © Grace Osborne, 2016

The right of Tony Ward to be identified as the Author
of this work has been asserted in accordance with the
Copyright, Designs and Patents Act 1988.

British Library Cataloguing in Publication Data.
A catalogue record for this book is available from the British Library.

ISBN 978 0 7509 6824 9

Typesetting and origination by The History Press
Printed in Great Britain

CONTENTS

ACKNOWLEDGEMENTS

Thanks firstly to Jenny Mark-Bell, editor of *Sussex Life*, who made space for my idea for a series with a new twist on local history. Now in its third year, this provided the impetus for *Unravelling Sussex*. Thanks also to my constant supporter, Vera Morley, and her book group who have fun puzzling out the solutions to my monthly riddles. Without the encouragement of her late husband Mike, an inspirational teacher, there would have been no poetry.

Thank you to my readers – particularly to those with connections to the subjects of my pieces who emailed me with such personal and positive responses. It makes it all worthwhile.

Thanks to Nicola Guy and all at The History Press for the encouragement, guidance and the Christmas card, and thanks to Mike Sims, the Poetry Society publishing manager, for the feature on my 'innovative project' in *Poetry News*. Hopefully other writers may feel inspired to join in with 'unravelling' their counties.

Thanks to my old friend, the late Peter Roget, whose *Thesaurus* still comes to the rescue in those early mornings when I'm searching for just the right word. And finally, thanks to my wife Sheila, both for her tolerance and for our extensive book collection, built up in the course of her lifelong love affair with history and literature, an invaluable resource.

ABOUT THE AUTHOR

Tony Ward was published regularly in various poetry magazines in his youth, and then enjoyed a successful career in computing and education. Now retired, he has returned to writing, combining poetry with his love of local history in a novel way. He lives in Eastbourne and is very much a Sussex person. He is a member of the Eastbourne Old Grammarians Association and a writer member of the Sussex Book Club. An Eastbourne Book Group run 'puzzle-sessions' using his Sussex Life series.

Tony will be donating a share of his royalties to St Wilfrid's Hospice, Eastbourne.

INTRODUCTION

Sussex is a county steeped in history. This book is a celebration of its cultural and artistic heritage through its much-loved places and some of the famous people who found inspiration here. You will find half-remembered poems and extracts from the novels, letters and diaries of well-known writers who had connections with Sussex. The county was also home to artists, actors, inventors, engineers, scientists, revolutionaries, explorers, sportsmen, a king and a saint. Surprising, amusing, heart-warming and heart-rending insights and anecdotes add to established fact. Sussex is a county of romance, but also, at times, tragedy.

As hinted at in the title, *Unravelling Sussex*, there is a new twist in this book's approach. If you wish, you can try a bit of puzzle solving. Each famous Sussex person or place is introduced by a riddle in the form of a poem. But this is no ordinary poem. The challenge is to unravel the embedded clues, which are then explained in the chapter that follows. It is poetry as *University Challenge*, pub quiz, or cryptic crossword. This will be familiar to followers of my monthly 'Poetry+' series in *Sussex Life* magazine.

If you are not into puzzles, just relax and enjoy an intriguing journey through Sussex. There is much to explore – historic sites and buildings, inspirational gardens, art collections and of course the natural beauty of the Sussex countryside.

If, upon completing the book, you would like to explore further, this is provided in the final section, the 'Explorer's Guide'. In this you will find both general advice and specific sources to follow up for each chapter. These include both print and website references, including audio/video clips. Assuming that you have website access, do call up some of the latter – they add a further enjoyable dimension.

As a taster, just some of the things you will discover by 'unravelling Sussex':

1 How a famous author spent his Nobel Prize money.
2 The novel by a Sussex resident upon which
   Andrew Lloyd-Webber based a musical.
3 The whereabouts of a stage designer's curtained TV set –
   a miniature theatre.
4 Who was found hiding in a windmill after losing a historic battle.
5 The person whose contribution was said to have
   shortened the Second World War by two years.
6 The setting for a late-in-life love match between a friend
   of the Prince Regent and his own dairy maid.
7 The writer who played ten first-class matches for the MCC (Marylebone
   Cricket Club), upon one occasion taking the wicket of W.G. Grace.
8 The inventor of a device whose widespread introduction was held up
   because it was thought it would really corrupt and ruin the nation!
9 The revolutionary whose writings played a major part
   in Great Britain losing its American colonies.
10 The explorer who 'never learned much geography at school'.
11 The setting in which you could have listened to the music of Gustav
   Holst, Leonard Bernstein, Pink Floyd, Bob Geldof and the Hollies.
12 The dutiful wife who held a castle against a siege
   while her husband was away fighting.
13 The scientist who duetted on piano with Albert Einstein on violin.
14 The event that gave birth to the novel *Frankenstein*.
15 The location of the Sixpenny Room.
16 The poet and artist who was inspired by Sussex's 'green and pleasant land'.
17 The location of no 'crouching tigers', but many 'hidden dragons'.

Please, read on …

EAST
SUSSEX

'THAT'S SHE!'

Young hands reached out to the donkeys,
much loved, but sadly no longer there.
Old hands get flour from the watermill,
through the almost wild garden.
Not a jungle though, no Mowgli.
Though still not made
'By singing, "Oh, how beautiful!" and sitting in the shade'.

The citation too, edged with flowers.
The prize money added yews and roses,
bought the children laughter –
a boating pond, a paddle boat.

And the house …
'That's She! The Only She! Make an honest woman of her – Quick!'
Perfect – our dream too!
But Carrie got there first.
If.

BATEMAN'S

FAMILY HOME OF RUDYARD KIPLING

Bateman's was Rudyard Kipling's seventeenth-century Wealden ironmaster's house, built in 1634 and purchased by him in 1902 as a family home for his wife and children. Rudyard Kipling (1865–1936) moved his family from 'The Elms', a rented house in Rottingdean, partly to escape the intrusion of sightseers. He lived at Bateman's until his death in January 1936. The National Trust acquired the house in 1939 after the death of Kipling's wife, Caroline (Carrie). The trust has left the house as it was in their lifetimes, including Kipling's book-lined study and writing desk.

A pair of donkeys used to live in the field on the hill alongside Bateman's. They were very friendly and came to be stroked, a high point for visiting children. In the grounds is a working watermill where stoneground flour can be purchased. It is reached by walking through a partly naturalised garden with wild flowers.

The 'jungle' is a reference to *The Jungle Book*, whose central character was the young boy Mowgli. Some relevant extracts follow. The discovery of Mowgli in the jungle by the Wolf Pack:

> 'A man's cub. Look!'
>   Directly in front of him, holding on to a low branch, stood a naked brown baby who could just walk – as soft and as dimpled a little thing as ever came to a wolf's cave at night. He looked up into Father Wolf's face and laughed.

Skip ten or eleven whole years:

> He grew up with the cubs, though they of course were grown wolves almost before he was a child, and Father Wolf taught him his business, and the meaning of things in the jungle, till every rustle in the grass, every breath of the warm night air, every note of the owls above his head, every scratch of a bat's claws as it roosted for a while in a tree, and every splash of every little fish jumping in a pool, meant just as much to him as the work of his office means to a business man.

The quote 'Oh, how beautiful!' is from Kipling's poem *The Glory of the Garden*, much reproduced on garden ornaments! Pennard Plants and the horticultural charity Roots and Shoots created an Edwardian themed garden in the Great Pavilion entitled 'The Glory of the Garden' for the May 2015 RHS Chelsea Flower Show to celebrate the 150th anniversary of Rudyard Kipling's birth.

'The citation' refers to his 1907 Nobel Prize for Literature Diploma citation, on view in the house. The Nobel Prize was awarded to Rudyard Kipling 'in consideration of the power of observation, originality of imagination, virility of ideas and remarkable talent for narration which characterise the creations of this world-famous author'. Each Nobel Prize Diploma incorporates a uniquely commissioned illustration – Kipling's is a particularly beautiful flower picture. As well as the diploma, each winner receives a gold medal and a sum of money. Kipling received £7,700, a significant amount in 1907, but far less in real terms than recent prize-winners. He and his wife decided to spend it on the garden. They planted the yew hedges and rose garden and had a shallow boating pond constructed complete with specially built paddle boat for their children and their friends.

When Kipling and his wife, Carrie, first saw Bateman's they fell in love with it instantly, hence Carrie's exclamation, 'That's She!'.

The final word, 'If', refers not just to most visitors' dream of themselves living in such a house, but to Kipling's perhaps most famous poem, *If*. This was written at Bateman's in 1910 and published in *Rewards and Fairies*. It spoke to parents all over the world. Sadly, Kipling's own son John was killed in the First World War at the Battle of Loos in 1915, five years later. John was 18 years of age.

In his foreword to *The Nation's Favourite Poems*, published by the BBC following a 1995 poll, Griff Rhys Jones reports that Kaiser Wilhelm II (Emperor of Germany during the First World War) was said to keep a copy of the poem on his desk. The desk in question was not in Germany, but in Holland after his abdication in 1918. The two men, on opposite sides in the Great War, suffered the same bereavement. The kaiser's own youngest son had committed suicide in 1920 and two of his grandsons were killed in the Second World War. Kipling's poem rose above partisan viewpoints to connect powerfully with universal aspirations.

The poem *If* was the clear winner, by twice as many votes as the runner-up, in the Nation's Favourite Poems poll. The extracts below quote some oft-remembered lines, including the first and last:

> If you can keep your head when all about you
> Are losing theirs and blaming it on you,
>
> If you can meet with Triumph and Disaster
> And treat those two imposters just the same;
>
> Yours is the Earth and everything that's in it,
> And – which is more –you'll be a Man, my son!

A HUNDRED MILES TO GO

Stars of stage and screen,
painted, filmed, photographed,
each brother bedazzled.

Their guiding light lost,
but regained,
restored.

Where the chalk wall falls to the foam,
children are rock-pooling through the ages,
countless ages,
encased in stones and bones.
Shrimping nets replace flint tools,
a new tribe
replacing the old.

And memories –
bluebirds over white cliffs,
where wings of war set forth.

Gap years in cottages, lost to time and tide.
Smoke still rising –
but now from happy driftwood fires,
evenings under the stars,
but still, for some, a hundred miles to go.

BEACHY HEAD, BIRLING GAP & THE SEVEN SISTERS

The Seven Sisters cliffs have been painted many times by both professional and amateur artists. They are also favourite photographic subjects for magazines, holiday snaps and for film locations, appearing in films as diverse as *Chitty Chitty Bang Bang, Robin Hood: Prince of Thieves, Harry Potter and the Goblet of Fire, Brighton Rock* and even a James Bond film, *The Living Daylights*.

'Each brother bedazzled' refers to the 1954 musical film *Seven Brides for Seven Brothers*, nominated in that year for Best Picture Oscar and the fifth most popular film at the British box office in 1955. There have been several stage adaptations since.

'Their guiding light lost' refers to the Belle Tout Lighthouse, overlooking the Seven Sisters on the clifftop near Beachy Head. However, this was not the first warning light to be set up. The first lights were located in 'Parson Darby's Hole'. Between the late 1600s and until his death in 1726, Parson Darby saved many lives. One of Parson Darby's duties, as parson of Friston and East Dean, was to bury the bodies washed up on the shore. Although some disasters were due to storms, others would have been due to the activities of wreckers luring them onto the rocks with misleading lights. Parson Darby set about establishing a reliable, fixed light. He excavated existing caverns near the base of the cliffs, creating ledges upon which he set lights on stormy nights. He kept watch throughout the night. Even if they should be driven onto the rocks, some sailors were saved by being pulled into 'Parson Darby's Hole'. Parson Darby's grave is in East Dean Churchyard. His epitaph reads, 'He was the sailors' friend.'

The Belle Tout Lighthouse, the first permanent 'guiding light', was built in 1828. The clifftop, however, was not a good location. Frequently shrouded in mist and constantly threatened with collapse due to recurrent cliff falls, it was decommissioned in 1899. It was not demolished, although in the Second World War it was seriously damaged as a result of being used for artillery target practice. After the war it was rebuilt as a private house. Inexorably though, cliff falls continued. In 1998, a successful major fundraising drive paid for the building to be moved intact, on rails, further back from the cliff edge. By then the 30ft safety margin in front of the house had collapsed into the sea. The cliffs are still eroding at an average of 1m per year.

The Belle Tout was used as the main location for the 1987 BAFTA award-winning drama series, *The Lives and Loves of a She Devil*, a BBC dramatisation of Fay Weldon's 1983 novel:

Mary Fisher lives in a High Tower, on the edge of the sea: she writes a great deal about the nature of love. She tells lies.

　　(The opening paragraph of *The Life and Loves of a She Devil*, by Fay Weldon.)

It is now a holiday let.

'But regained ...' refers to the replacement Beachy Head Lighthouse built at the foot of the cliffs which was brought into service in 1902. 'Restored' refers to this lighthouse nearly losing its iconic red and white stripes when Trinity House announced in October 2011 that it could no longer afford to repaint them. The lighthouse would have been left to return to its natural granite grey. A widely supported fundraising campaign avoided this fate by reaching the repainting target of £27,000 in July 2013. The repainting by a specialist team, including two abseilers, took just under three weeks, being completed on 9 October 2013. The campaign had attracted worldwide support. Notable supporters and donors included Eddie Izzard, the Duke of Devonshire, Ronda and David Armitage (who respectively wrote and illustrated *The Lighthouse Keeper* books for children), Bill Bryson, Griff Rhys Jones, John Craven (a BBC *Countryfile* item) and many local organisations and individuals.

When the Beachy Head Lighthouse was manned, up until 1983, there used to be a cable strung from the clifftop to the platform encircling the top of the lighthouse, just below the light. During construction of the lighthouse (1900–02) twin heavy-duty cables were installed for a temporary cable car to take workers and building materials to an iron platform installed next to the lighthouse site. These were removed, but a connection was retained to carry a telephone cable. This was before the days of mobile phones. The cable is no longer there.

David Armitage, who illustrated his wife's *Lighthouse Keeper* books, tells how the presence of the cable provided the idea for the first book. One day, in the late 1970s, when a cable was still in place, David was walking on the clifftop with their children, Joss and Kate. As young children are wont to do, he was asked, 'Daddy, what is that cable for?'

David had an inspiration, 'Well, that is to send the lighthouse keeper his lunch.'

The first book was, of course, called *The Lighthouse Keeper's Lunch*. First published in 1977 by Andre Deutsch Ltd, it was an immediate prize-winner, being awarded the Esther Glen Award for Best Book of the Year (New Zealand, 1978). It was the first of Ronda's series of nine bestselling books, now modern classics. It tells of how 'Mr Grinling gets his lunch in a most peculiar way'.

On her website Ronda tells 'all about me'. New Zealand was her birthplace and it was her home until soon after completing her teacher training. At the age of 23 she took ship for England. She met David, a Tasmanian, on the ship. They married in England, travelled for a while and then in 1974 settled permanently in Sussex. The books continue to be bestselling, much-loved favourites of young children and their teachers, widely used in primary schools. A thirtieth anniversary edition was brought out in 2007 by the current publishers, Scholastic Children's Books.

Turning our attention to the beach, 'Where the chalk wall falls to the foam' is a line from the poem *Seascape*, by W.H. Auden. The complete poem is engraved on a brass plaque on a memorial bench beside a path called the 'Friston Drencher' to be found on the OS Explorer Map of Eastbourne and Beachy Head. This path leads from the South Downs Way above Jevington towards the Seven Sisters. The complete poem beautifully encapsulates the essence of the view:

> Here at the small field's ending pause
> Where the chalk wall falls to the foam, and its tall ledges
> Oppose the pluck
> And knock of the tide,
> And the shingle scrambles after the suck-
> ing surf,
> And the gull lodges
> A moment on its sheer side.

(*Seascape*, by W.H. Auden, Verse 2 of 3.)

'Rock-pooling' and fossil hunting are two of the activities put on by the National Trust at Birling Gap. Stone-age flint tools, ten thousand years old, have also been discovered at this location, whose name derives from that of the Saxon tribe who settled there – 'Baerlingas'.

In the Second World War the cliffs and lighthouses were used as a landmark for bombers bound for Germany and for fighters returning to their bases. For many bomber crews, shot down on their missions, Beachy Head was their last sight of England. This sad reflection is now inscribed on a memorial on the clifftop. The inspirational Vera Lynn's wartime song contains the line 'There'll be blue birds over the white cliffs of Dover'. As the real white cliffs of Dover are no longer white, cliff falls there having been halted, the Seven Sisters cliffs often stand in for them in films, TV and even the Dover Town Council publicity website!

'Gap years in cottages, lost to time and tide' remembers, for many, holidays spent in the row of holiday cottages at Birling Gap. The cottages are gradually disappearing over the cliff due to erosion. Before the days of portable barbecues, both locals and holidaymakers gathered up driftwood on the beach to make fires for 'sausage sizzles', often in the evenings, when the sparks from the fire flew up to the stars. Come morning, South Downs Way walkers still had the best part of 100 miles to go to reach the end of the long-distance footpath near Winchester.

AN OAK LEAF ON THE BEAM

Pride of a survivor,
but a humbler house than the cathedral next door,
property of the priory,
five hundred years,
but fallen from grace.

The pleading voice heard,
guardian angels, patron saints,
reformer, vicar, lawyer.
Ten pounds bought new life
and an oak leaf on a beam.
Restored to grace,
Survivor.

Survivors too in the garden.
Beside the reeded riverbank,
Forbidden fruit, forgotten fruit,
mulberry, medlar, betrayer –
blood on its branches.

One hundred years on,
the ten-pound purchase celebrated –
a sundial, a bridge from the past,
a rose for the founder, a battle now won,
telling their stories to days yet to come.

3

ALFRISTON CLERGY HOUSE
THE FIRST BUILDING PURCHASED
BY THE NATIONAL TRUST

Alfriston Clergy House was the first building purchased, in 1896, by the newly formed National Trust (the very first acquisition had been 5 acres of clifftop at Dinas Oleu in Wales). The vendors were the Ecclesiastical Commissioners, the house having been in the ownership of the nearby Michelham Priory for the previous 500 years. The purchase price was £10, a nominal sum even in today's equivalent, but necessary to satisfy the legal requirements of the sale.

Next door to the 'humbler house' stands the Church of St Andrew, known as the 'Cathedral of the South Downs'. The fourteenth-century church was built around ten years after the Clergy House in the shape of a Greek cross with a central bell tower. The bells are rung from the floor of the chancel crossing, in full view of the congregation.

The Clergy House, a thatched, timber-framed Wealden 'hall house', was not originally built by the Church. It was built in 1350, the 'pride of a survivor' – a yeoman farmer who prospered after the Black Death. By reducing the working population by up to one third, this had increased the wages and profit margins of the survivors. It wasn't until 1395 that the priory was able to add the house to its extensive estates. The term 'clergy house' refers to its ownership by the Church, not because a priest lived there.

Upon exploring the house – warning, low doorways – and passing through the sixteenth-century parlour into the main two-storey high hall, it is the floor that is worthy of note. It is composed of a pounded down mixture of ground chalk and sour milk, a locally available and eco-friendly alternative to concrete. An information sheet even shows the chemical reaction involved, complete with chemical equations.

Over the next 500 years the house was modified and extended several times. Tenants came and went, but by 1885 the house had become a liability and the Church authorities sought permission to demolish it once the existing elderly occupant, Harriet Coates, had died. This happened three years later.

However, the local vicar, the Reverend F.W. Beynon, campaigned vigorously to save the house. In one initiative, the Reverend Beynon contacted a group of three friends who, first separately and then together, were deeply committed to saving unspoilt countryside and ancient buildings threatened with destruction. The three like-minded campaigners were Octavia Hill, Canon Hardwicke Rawnsley and Sir Robert Hunter.

The 'reformer' in the poem is Octavia Hill (1838–1912), the eighth daughter among twelve children who, starting work at the age of 14, had tirelessly devoted herself to social reform. She was shocked by the terrible living conditions of the poor East End children in 'the raggedy school' where she helped out. Funded by John Ruskin, who acquired the leases, she set about renovating and letting out previously rundown houses. In a short time she had fifteen housing schemes under her management with around 3,000 tenants.

'Open space for all' was another campaign, successfully leading to the acquisition of Parliament Hill Fields and Hampstead Heath through the Commons Preservation Society. As Octavia Hill entreated, 'We all need space; unless we have it we cannot reach that sense of quiet in which whispers of better things come to us gently ...'. Octavia Hill was the first person to use the phrase 'Green Belt'.

The 'vicar' in the poem is Canon Hardwicke Rawnsley (1851–1920). With the support of the others he had successfully campaigned to stop the construction of railways to serve slate quarries in some of the most beautiful parts of the Lake District.

The third member of the group, the 'lawyer' in the poem, is Sir Robert Hunter (1844–1913), who was to become the first chairman of the executive committee of what he christened 'The National Trust for Places of Historic Interest or Natural Beauty'. Being a bit of a mouthful, this was shortened to the National Trust. As the lawyer in the group, it was Hunter who had first formulated the proposal for a society to protect land (and subsequently properties) and who secured its permanent status by drafting the Bill which became the 1907 National Trust Act:

> The central idea is that of a Land Company, formed not for the promotion of thrift or the spread of political principles, and not primarily for profit, but with a view to the protection of the public interest in open spaces in the country ... the acquisition and holding of properties ... the acquisition of manors ... and the maintenance and management of gardens ... as places of resort for recreation and instruction. (From a speech given by Sir Robert Hunter at the National Association for the Promotion of Social Science in Birmingham, September 1884.)

One of the first actions of the trust was the launching of the successful appeal by Octavia Hill for funds to restore Alfriston Clergy House, which by then (1895) was in a dreadful state of repair. The phrase 'the pleading voice' and the last line of the poem are taken from Octavia's text, 'the pleading voice of the old building itself ... to be left to tell its story to the days that are to come'. She promoted Alfriston Clergy House as 'rich in memories of England as our ancestors knew'.

On the corner of a beam in the original hall of the house is a spot-lit carving of an oak leaf. It is thought that this may have been the original inspiration for the National Trust's emblem.

Outside, the garden, largely laid out by the first National Trust tenant Sir Robert Witt in the 1920s, is bordered by the River Cuckmere. The garden surrounds the house. It is not a large garden in National Trust terms but contains some interesting features and artefacts. There is a medieval-style box garden, roses chosen for their scent, a medieval herb garden, and a productive vegetable garden laid out as a series of eight raised beds retained with railway sleepers.

The orchard contains old 'forbidden fruit' apple varieties like Sussex Duck's Bill, Lady Henniker, Lady Sudeley, Crawley Beauty and the local Alfriston. Also, perhaps 'forgotten fruit', are the mulberry and medlar trees. The 'betrayer – blood on its branches' refers to the Judas tree (*Cercis siliquastrum*), so called because it was a tree of this Mediterranean species from which Judas Iscariot is believed to have hung himself. Its clusters of dark pink flowers appearing around Easter time on bare branches are traditionally said to resemble drops of blood.

A walnut tree is a favourite of the squirrels, and the garden is also home to a large variety of birds, whatever the season. These include green and great spotted woodpeckers, kingfishers, tree creepers and a sparrowhawk. The trust also puts on 'bat evenings'.

In 1995, the centenary of the National Trust was celebrated with the installation of a special sundial, sitting on a balustrade from the old London Waterloo Bridge, 'a bridge from the past'.

Octavia Hill's vital role in the founding of the National Trust was also celebrated by the naming of a new rose variety in her honour. Octavia Hill and her two fellow campaigners, through their dedication and tenacity, accomplished the seemingly impossible – 'a battle now won'. The National Trust continues 'telling their stories to days yet to come'.

BRIGHT LIGHTS

Bright lights of London forsaking bright lights of London,
a quieter beacon brings together the dancing partners.

Sisters off the beaten track that binds them.

The artist,
paint on the canvas, paint on the walls, the chairs, the tables,
a house of youth, breaking conventions, forging bonds –
new ideas for a new world.

The writer,
blue streams flowing from her pen in a room of her own,
the house a mongrel who stole her heart,
good days,
'bells ringing for church – daffodils out – apple trees in blossom –
cows mooing – cocks crowing – thrushes chirping ...'

But an idyll stolen by the black dog,
the bad days,
the sounds not heard, the sights not seen,
weighed down, carried away
not now by streams of thought,
but by the force of an unyielding tide.

4

CHARLESTON AND MONK'S HOUSE

HOMES OF THE SISTERS VANESSA BELL AND VIRGINIA WOOLF

Charleston Farmhouse, at Firle near Lewes, and the nearby Monk's House (National Trust), at Rodmell near Lewes, were the East Sussex retreats of the two sisters. They were both members of the Bloomsbury Group, a close-knit group of artists, writers and intellectuals who first came to prominence in the First World War. Originally centred on the Bloomsbury area of London, they used these 'oases of calm' to escape from their hectic London lives. The permanent residents of Charleston, at various times from 1916 onwards, were the artists Vanessa Bell and Duncan Grant, together with Bell's two children, Julian and Quentin. Also resident during the First World War was the writer David Garnett. Grant and Garnett, both conscientious objectors and lovers, were required to work on the land. Although Vanessa's husband, Clive, was a regular visitor and indeed moved into a set of rooms in the house just before the Second World War, their marriage had long been one in name only. On Christmas Day 1918, Vanessa and Duncan's daughter, Angelica, was born at the house, completing a household that broke the conventions of the day.

Visitors included writers and critics – T.S. Eliot, E.M. Forster, Lytton Strachey, David Garnett and Vita Sackville-West (also of Sissinghust garden fame); artists and art critics – Roger Fry and Clive Bell; and the economists Saxon Sidney Turner and Maynard Keynes. 'The house seems full of young people in very high spirits ...' (Vanessa Bell, 1936).

The group as a whole had a 'desire to break with the Victorian past', both in their work and their domestic arrangements. This was even further in evidence when David Garnett, who had been present at the birth of Angelica Bell, wrote to a friend that he thought that he may marry her, 'when she is 20, I shall be 46 – will it be scandalous'. True to his word, on 8 May 1942 they married – she was 23, he was 49. Garnett's novel, *Aspects of Love* (1955), was the basis for the Andrew Lloyd-Webber musical of the same name.

Charleston had been discovered by Virginia Woolf, who had bought a house with her husband Leonard in Lewes. Virginia was keen for her sister to also have a place nearby and wrote to Vanessa, 'If you lived there you could make it absolutely divine'. Vanessa and Duncan wasted no time and took out a lease on the house – 'It's most lovely, very solid and simple ...'

There's a wall of trees – one single line of elms all round two sides ... We are just below Firle Beacon ... Inside the house the rooms are very large ... Ten bedrooms I think some enormous. One I shall make into a studio. The Omega dinner service looks most lovely in the dresser.

(Letter from Vanessa Bell to Roger Fry.)

Vanessa died at Charleston on 7 April 1961, aged 81, but the family kept a lease on the property until after Duncan's death in 1978. The house is now in the care of the Charleston Trust who opened it to the public in 1986, following an initial period of restoration. Already a highly successful living museum, the ambitious Charleston Centenary Project (1916–2016) will further extend this work.

A particular feature of the property are the works of art. Vanessa and Duncan not only painted pictures on canvas or board, but extensively decorated the walls, doors and furniture. They also filled the house with ceramics, textiles, paintings by other artists of the time and objects from the Omega Workshops. The latter was set up by the artist and art critic Roger Fry in 1913 to provide his artist friends with a regular income.

In the poem, a reference to the name of the house is in the second line – 'dancing partners'. The Charleston was the name of a dance popular in the 1920s and first featured in the Broadway show *Runnin' Wild* (1923) – perhaps also considered a feature of some of the Bloomsbury set!

Charleston was connected to Monk's House by 'the beaten track' known as the South Downs Way. Door to door it is about a 5-mile fairly strenuous walk. Virginia Woolf regularly walked over to see her sister, but sometimes found it hard going. In her diary entry for 12 November 1939 she wrote, 'I walked seven miles alone to Charleston & suffer for it'. She didn't always have much luck cycling either; on another occasion she writes, 'bicycled round there in a flood of rain'.

Although Virginia and Leonard Woolf had recently purchased a house in Lewes (the Round House), they were intrigued by a notice in a local auctioneer's, 'Lot 1. Monk's House, Rodmell. An old-fashioned house standing in three quarters of an acre of land.' Although first impressions of the house, a seventeenth-century small, weather-boarded cottage, were not entirely positive, they fell in love with 'the size & shape & fertility & wildness of the garden'. On 1 July 1919, in a nail-biting auction, they secured their dream with a winning bid of £700.

The house was to become an essential part of Virginia Woolf's life 'after the fashion of a mongrel who wins your heart'. Decorated in like manner to Charleston by Vanessa and Duncan, Monk's House became another home-from-home for the Bloomsbury Group. 'I feel so intensely the delights of shutting oneself up in a little world of one's own, with pictures and music and everything beautiful' (*The Voyage Out*, Virginia Woolf, 1915).

Virginia Woolf's famous writing room is at the bottom of the garden next to an undulating lawn where they played bowls. As she urged in her 1929 book-length essay, *A Room of One's Own*, 'a woman must have money and a room of her own if she is to write fiction'. The 'blue streams' in the poem refer to the fact that she favoured blue writing paper.

The 'good days' and 'bad days' of the poem refer to Virginia's bipolar disorder, a mental condition then termed 'manic depression' in which sufferers experience extreme mood swings from euphoria (good days) to deep depression (bad days – for which Sir Winston Churchill blamed his own 'black dog'). The 'good days' quote – 'bells ringing ... thrushes chirping ...' – is taken verbatim from Virginia's letter to her sister written on Good Friday, 2 April 1920. Good days – days of optimism with Leonard at Monk's House – were also perhaps reflected in her writing:

> Yet Byron never made tea as you do, who fill the pot so that when you put the lid on the tea spills over. There is a brown pool on the table – it is running among your books and papers. Now you mop it up, clumsily, with your pocket handkerchief. You then stuff your handkerchief back in your pocket – that is not Byron; that is so essentially you that if I think of you in twenty years' time, when we are both famous, gouty and intolerable, it will be by that scene: and if you are dead, I shall weep. (*The Waves*, Virginia Woolf, 1931.)

The Woolfs immersed themselves in village life and Virginia's final novel, *Between the Acts* (1941), is full of references to Rodmell village life.

Sadly, the book was published posthumously. The 'bad days' won out. On 28 March 1941 she put on an overcoat, weighed down her pockets with stones, walked into the nearby tidal River Ouse and drowned herself. Leonard found her stick on the bank near the swing bridge at Southease, but her body was not found until three weeks later:

> Dearest.
> I feel certain that I am going mad again. I feel we can't go through another of these terrible times. And I shan't recover this time. I begin to hear voices, and I can't concentrate. So I am doing what seems the best thing to do. You have given me the greatest possible happiness. You have been in every way all that anyone could be. I don't think two people could have been happier 'til this terrible disease came. I can't fight any longer. I know that I am spoiling your life, that without me you could work. And you will I know. You see I can't even write this properly. I can't read. What I want to say is I owe all the happiness of my life to you. You have been entirely patient with me and incredibly good. I want to say that – everybody knows it. If anybody could have saved me it would have been you. Everything has gone from me but the certainty of your goodness. I can't go on spoiling your life any longer. I don't think two people could have been happier than we have been. (Virginia Woolf's handwritten suicide note to her husband Leonard.)

The 'stream of consciousness' literary style which she had made famous in her novels, *Mrs Dalloway* (1925) and *To the Lighthouse* (1927), had become an all too real river of death.

Following her cremation, Leonard buried her ashes under one of two elm trees (now gone) on the edge of the bowling lawn. His ashes were to join hers under the other elm in 1969. The inscription on Virginia Woolf's grave, chosen by Leonard, was taken from the end of her novel, *The Waves* – 'Against you I will fling myself, unvanquished and unyielding, O Death!'

FOOTHOLD

A Roman fort of the Saxon Shore,
lapped by a tidal lagoon, long gone.
A harbour for a Channel fleet, no more …
retreat, resettlement, massacre.
Abandoned.

A Norman foothold to conquer a nation,
the shelter before the storm,
the unfolding tapestry.
Two weeks to a place in history
on Senlac field.

And after … the castle rebuilt, the ruins restored,
a castle within a castle, permanence, power.

Five hundred years,
Four times besieged, four times rebels,
Twice surrendered but never captured,
and next, a noble prison, a new role.
James, Edward, Joan – a King, a Duke, a Queen
fallen from favour into dungeon gloom.

And still the guardian,
Tudor cannons await a Spanish fleet,
machine gun posts define another war,
another threat.

And what remains …
stone balls, a cannon, a stump of Keep
whose walls now shield no more than sheep.

5

PEVENSEY CASTLE

WILLIAM THE CONQUEROR'S FOOTHOLD BEFORE THE BATTLE OF HASTINGS

Pevensey Castle is a medieval castle and former Roman 'Saxon Shore' fort in the care of English Heritage. The site is a scheduled monument, open to visitors.

The Roman fort's name was *Anderitum*, as listed in *The Notitia Dignitatum* (List of High Offices). This document includes the names of military stations in Britain at the end of the fourth century AD. Anderitum was the garrison of an infantry unit of the Roman border forces (*Numerus Abulcorum*). The original name also sometimes appears in later publications as *Anderita* or *Anderida*. The name Pevensey Castle strictly refers to the later medieval castle built in one corner of the site of the Roman fort.

The *Notitia* lists Anderitum as one of nine 'forts of the Saxon Shore' (*Litus Saxonicum*), stretching from Brancaster, near the Wash in East Anglia, to Portchester Castle near Portsmouth. Portchester is the next fort to Pevensey and the last in the chain. The forts were built between about AD 260 and AD 300. At around AD 290, Anderitum was one of the last and largest to be built. Another two or three forts, together with intermediate watchtowers, are sometimes also included in the group. However, there is some academic discussion as to whether they were an integrated defensive system on both sides of the Channel, against Saxon raiders, or whether they served some other purpose. The label 'Saxon Shore' certainly conjures up a memorable image though! It has even been taken as the name of an American band!

'Lapped by a tidal lagoon' refers to the fact that the fort was originally on a peninsula surrounded on three sides by a tidal lagoon and marshes, a very strong defensive position. There is also evidence that there was a harbour, which could have been a base for the Romans' Channel Fleet (*Classis Britannica*). The lagoon has long since silted up and the marshes have been drained. There is no trace of the harbour. Pevensey Castle is now landlocked, about a mile from the sea.

'Retreat, resettlement, massacre' refers to the years after the Roman Army retreated from Britain by AD 410. The local population moved onto the site and used it as a trading base. The curtain walls of the old fort provided some protection from Saxon raiders until AD 491 (but possibly AD 471, due to a dating error) when the *Anglo-Saxon Chronicle* refers to a massacre in which the Saxons 'Aella and Cyssa besieged Anderida [Andredesceaster] and killed all who were inside, so there was not one Briton left' (from Anne Savage's illustrated modern translation). Aella became King of Sussex. He was obviously taking a leaf out of Marcus Aurelius Carausius' book (his predecessor, the Roman naval commander of Anderitum), who had fallen out with the Roman Emperor Maximian and declared himself ruler of an independent Britain. Mind you, Carausius had gone one better, his kingdom also included part of Northern Gaul.

The next man of ambition to arrive was of course William the Conqueror. Landing at Pevensey Bay on 28 September 1066, his army quickly constructed a temporary fortification within the old Roman fort – 'the shelter before the storm'. The 'storm' took place on 14 October 1066, just over two weeks later. The 'place in history on Senlac field' was of course the Battle of Hastings. The date has become perhaps the best remembered in our history. 'The unfolding tapestry' refers not only to the sequence of events but to their depiction in the Bayeux Tapestry.

In the century after the Conquest, the Normans built a full-scale castle within one corner of the site of the ruined Roman fort and repaired the outer Roman curtain walls. The next 500 years were not uneventful. The castle was besieged four times. It was well fortified though, and although 'twice surrendered' it was 'never captured'. The sieges were:

1088   Rebel barons defended Pevensey Castle against King William Rufus. They surrendered when their food ran out.

1147   Another rebellious owner, Gilbert de Clare, was besieged by another king, King Stephen, with the same result.

In the later medieval (Plantagenet kings) period, the castle was further rebuilt and strengthened. However, this proved no deterrent to attack:

1264–65 In the Second Baron's War, after the Battle of Lewes, defeated members of King Henry III's Royalist army fled to Pevensey and held out against Simon de Montfort's men for a year. This time they were able to get food supplies through the siege lines. De Montfort gave up in July 1265. One month later he was killed at the Battle of Evesham.

1399   While the constable of the castle, Sir John Pelham, was away fighting with Henry Bolingbroke, his wife, Lady Joan, held the castle against King Richard II's supporters. The siege failed. Upon Richard II's forced abdication, Bolingbroke was crowned King Henry IV.

During the siege, Lady Joan had written a heart-rending letter to her husband, a translated extract from which reads:

I am here bylaid in manner of a siege, with the counties of Sussex, Surrey and a great part of Kent, so that I may not out, nor no vitals get me without much difficulty. Wherefore my dear may it please you, by the advice of your wise council, to give remedy to the salvation of your castle … Farewell my dear Lord, the Holy Trinity keep you from your enemies, and soon send me good tidings of you. Written at Pevensey in the Castle, on Saint Jacob day last past. By ever your own poor, J. Pelham.

Lady Joan's ghost, the 'grey lady', is said to sometimes be seen pacing the parapet, scanning the horizon for her husband's return and the end of her ordeal.

Sir John Pelham was a key supporter, first of King Henry IV and then his successor King Henry V. This was on three counts. Firstly, Pevensey Castle was considered to be the safest prison in the kingdom, more secure than the Tower of London. Henry IV had placed 'the Mortimer boys' in close custody at Pevensey since the elder boy, Edmund Mortimer, had through descent from King Edward III, an arguably stronger claim to the throne than he did, and so also upon his death did his son. However, Henry IV's own son did succeed him, as Henry V. Following his father's lead, when Henry V needed to keep King James of Scotland in custody while he and most of his knights were about to leave for France, he also chose Pevensey Castle. He paid Sir John £700 annually to guard his captive.

The second connection was that Sir John was obviously good with money. He was one of two 'war treasurers' who held the cash voted by Parliament for Henry IV's military expeditions and a few years later Henry handed over the seal of the exchequer to him. His last duty for Henry IV, following his death in 1413, was to act as one of the executors of his will. In the case of Henry V, Sir John didn't continue as the top 'money man'. However, he still had an important role to play. He acted as security for some of the loans raised by the king and his retinue to pay for his very expensive French campaign. He was also the recipient of at least one private 'begging letter':

> Right worshipful and worthy Sir, you will want to know that I am here, and have been at great costs and expense, wherefore I need to borrow a notable sum before I go and fare from my house ... [I place] full hope and trust in your gracious and gentle person to help and succour me at this time in my greatest necessity, to lend me some notable sum of gold ... Written in haste at Southampton, the 12th day of July [1415].
>
> (From 'John Cheney, a royal esquire of the body', quoted in Ian Mortimer, *1415 Henry V's Year of Glory*.)

The third reason for Sir John's friendship with two successive monarchs was that he was a comrade in arms to both. In the case of Henry V, most notably this was at the Battle of Agincourt on 25 October 1415, Saint Crispin's Day:

> We few, we happy few, we band of brothers;
> For he to-day that sheds his blood with me
> Shall be my brother;
>
> (William Shakespeare, *Henry V*, Act 4, Scene 3.)

'And next, a noble prison, a new role' – as previously mentioned, the Lancastrian kings used the castle as a secure prison for high-ranking nobles. As well as 'the Mortimer boys' and King James I of Scotland (captured on his way to France in 1406), these included Edward of Norwich, 2nd Duke of York (for plotting against King Henry IV), and Queen Joan of Navarre, Henry IV's second wife (held from 1419 to 1422 on the orders of her stepson, Henry V, on a false charge of plotting to kill him through witchcraft).

There are two dungeons, both damp and gloomy. The oubliette (from the French *oublier* – 'to forget') is accessed by a trapdoor, and a separate dungeon is reached by a spiral staircase. In his will Edward of Norwich left £20 to his jailer, Thomas Playsted, 'for the kindness he showed me when I was in ward at Pevensey'. Unsurprisingly, kindness in such circumstances was to be highly valued. The Sussex Archaeology website notes the theory that Queen Joan is an alternative contender for the ghostly role of the 'grey lady'.

When the Tudors took over, the castle was abandoned, apart from the installation of two cannons at the time of the Spanish Armada in 1588. One of these cast-iron cannons, probably manufactured in a local Sussex Weald ironworks, is preserved in the inner bailey of the castle. It is mounted on a replica carriage, in turn inevitably mounted by children having their photos taken.

The castle's last private owner, the 9th Duke of Devonshire, gave the castle to the state in 1925 as a historic monument. The castle's most recent role – 'and still the guardian' – was in the Second World War when in 1940 it was reoccupied by the military against the threat of a German invasion after the fall of France. Machine-gun pillboxes were built into the fabric of the castle and anti-tank measures were installed. The space enclosed by the original Roman curtain walls, the outer bailey, was used as a training ground for the Home Guard in the Second World War. It is now shared between visitors and, occasionally, by grazing sheep.

'And what remains ...' – the pyramid of large stone balls near the 'stump of the keep' are fourteenth-century catapult (trebuchet) ammunition.

HERE BE DRAGONS

Lodging House, Villa, Palace,
Prince to King. Transformations.

Pleasure-seeker set free,
drinking, dining, dancing, gambling, racing,
a secret marriage, a sanctioned marriage
failed. Overspending, overeating,
bad image, bad press. *'Prince of Whales'*.

But a man of vision. *'A stately pleasure-dome'*,
pinnacles, minarets, towers,
chinoiserie, oriental fantasy.
A Prince's passion, but too soon
a King's lost world.

A change of players. Succession,
the younger brother, the faithful wife,
new brooms welcomed, accepted, liked,
but all too short a stay. Succession,
the niece, the consort. A change of tone,
too cramped a Palace, too much on view,
London by the sea. The Palace sold.

Purchased by the town. Refurnished,
refurbished, restored. Civic Pride.

East meets West. A sanctuary in time of war.
Wounded, tended, honoured,
the stricken sons of Empire.
Thanks. Gifts exchanged, a Gateway for a golden key,
and for the gift of life.

Altered, damaged, neglected, compensated.
Setbacks, fire and storm,
Restored anew, undaunted.
Firm favourite, film favourite,
a million feet now follow ghosts,
tracing footsteps of soldiers, of Emperors, of Kings.

6

THE ROYAL PAVILION, BRIGHTON
THE PRINCE REGENT'S SEASIDE RETREAT

The poem title suggested itself, and is in fact a quote. The phrase was originally used on early maps to indicate dangerous or unexplored territories.
In this context it has since been used by computer programmers to indicate
obscure passages of source code. It has also been taken up by writers and
filmmakers to signal fantastical places or happenings. The Royal Pavilion is
just such a fantasy.

There is extensive use of two-dimensional or three-dimensional dragons in
the decorative schemes throughout the palace, notably the Dragon Chandelier
in the Banqueting Room, 30ft high and weighing 1 ton!

Not all dragons are in plain sight though; in the Red Drawing Room they are
hidden in the wood-grain effect of doors and wood-panelled surfaces. All are
distinctly oriental in appearance and recall Tolkien's own illustration of Smaug
the dragon in his well-known book *The Hobbit*, in which we read:

> ... about him on all sides stretching away across unseen floors, lay countless piles
> of precious things, gold wrought and unwrought, gems and jewels, and silver red-
> stained in the ruddy light.

Not a bad description of the treasures in the Banqueting Room.

The writer of one section of the Pavilion's official website also picked up
on the dragon theme by entitling the section 'No crouching tigers, but many
hidden dragons'. The connection here is to the Academy award-winning martial
arts film *Crouching Tiger, Hidden Dragon* (2000), directed by Ang Lee and loosely
based on a book of the same name, one of a five-part series written between
1938 and 1942 by Wang Du Lu.

The most famous royal resident of the Royal Pavilion was the Prince of Wales,
who became Prince Regent in 1811 as his father, George III, was deemed inca-
pable of continuing with the duties of a monarch. Upon his father's death nine
years later, the Prince Regent succeeded him, as King George IV. George had
first visited Brighton in 1783, escaping from his stifling and disciplined upbringing and lodging in Grove House with his fast-living uncle, Prince Henry, Duke of
Cumberland. Within a few years he had bought a small place of his own.

In 1785 the 23-year-old Prince George married his true love, the 29-year-old
Catholic widow Mrs Maria Fitzherbert. This had to be 'a secret marriage'
because English law excluded Catholics from the throne. His 'sanctioned marriage', in the Chapel Royal at St James Palace, was to Caroline of Brunswick ten

years later. He agreed to this in order to write off his debts. The marriage failed within the year. Both partners had extra-marital affairs.

As regards the 'small place of his own', between 1787 and 1823 the original building underwent three major transformations, the final result being the Royal Pavilion that we know today, which is the work of the architect John Nash. The present Brighton Museum and Brighton Dome Concert Hall buildings were completed in 1808, as part of the second phase. They dwarfed the existing modest Marine Pavilion. They were originally a riding school and stable complex, designed by William Porden for the Prince Regent's sixty-two horses. The horses had more impressive accommodation than the prince.

That would not do. In 1815 the final phase, the transformation of the Marine Pavilion into his oriental palace, got under way. The work took eight years. A final touch was to link the stable complex by an underground passageway to the fantasy now dominating the site. This enabled King George, now sensitive about being seen by the public because of his obesity, to have direct and private access between his now necessary ground floor apartments and the stable complex.

George had a great interest in architecture and the fine and decorative arts. For his seaside retreat he was in favour of something exotic. He and his designers were heavily influenced by both Chinese (chinoiserie) and Indian styles, an alternative to the classical mainstream Regency style. Coincidentally, in 1816, as work started on the transformation of the Royal Pavilion into the 'oriental fantasy' we see today, Samuel Taylor Coleridge's poem *Kubla Khan* was published:

In Xanadu did Kubla Khan
A stately pleasure-dome decree

Was Brighton the Prince Regent's Xanadu?

George notoriously overspent and overate. He was accused of squandering money at a time when Britain was hugely in debt as a result of a war against France and many people were living in poverty. He hosted gastronomic feasts in the Banqueting Room with up to seventy dishes. As the Royal Pavilion and Museums' excellent official website explains, his French chef Marie Antonin Careme didn't just prepare meals, 'he created culinary works of art, including confectionary pieces four foot high by two foot across'. George was not known to hold back. George eventually became so obese that he couldn't manage the stairs and his apartments had to be relocated downstairs.

'Bad image, bad press' refers to the biting caricatures of the king and his circle of friends produced by James Gillray (1757–1815) and other satirists of the day. George Cruickshank's caricature of the grossly overweight Prince George portrays him as 'The Prince of Whales' (1812). The Royal Pavilion and Museums have a large collection of such caricatures, some on display in the Royal Pavilion.

George succeeded to the throne in 1820. The Royal Pavilion was completed three years later, but his ill health and the responsibilities of state conspired against him. He only made two further visits, in 1824 and 1827 – 'a king's lost world'. King George IV died in 1830, aged 68.

George's younger brother succeeded to the throne as William IV. He and Queen Adelaide took over the Royal Pavilion. They were 'new brooms welcomed, accepted, liked'. They made themselves more visible and their entertaining was more restrained and informal. No more formal gastronomic feasts for fellow kings and emperors. But 'all too short a stay', William IV died just seven years later, in 1837.

'Succession' – the throne now passed to William's niece. Queen Victoria made her first visit to her palace in 1837, the year of her uncle's death. She found it a 'strange, odd, Chinese looking place both outside and inside'. She returned in 1842, this time with her husband Prince Albert and two children. Neither the palace nor the town was to their liking. There wasn't enough space (the royal couple eventually ended up with nine children), and there was a lack of privacy – 'The people here are very indiscreet and troublesome.' Queen Victoria also liked to keep a tight hold on the purse strings and did not wish to be associated with such a monument to extravagance. She sold the palace to the Town of Brighton in 1850 for the sum of £53,000. Osborne House on the Isle of Wight became the family's summer home.

Brighton Council set about refurnishing, refurbishing and restoring the Royal Pavilion. It was a matter of 'Civic Pride' and also a major draw for the increasing numbers of visitors taking advantage of the London to Brighton Railway which had opened a few years before (1841) – 'London by the sea'. Over the years many of the items which had initially been removed from the palace by Queen Victoria were returned, firstly by Queen Victoria herself, then later by George V and Queen Mary, and in the mid-1950s on a permanent loan basis by our present Queen Elizabeth II. The Royal Pavilion had become a 'people's palace', to which, up until the 1920s, access was granted to anyone bearing a sixpenny piece.

The penultimate verse remembers the Royal Pavilion's role, between December 1914 and February 1916, as a hospital for soldiers of the Indian Army wounded on the Western Front. By 1914 the Indian Army provided almost one third of the British Expeditionary Force. The Royal Pavilion and adjacent buildings were adapted to accommodate over 600 beds. The Great Kitchen became one of two operating theatres. Over 2,000 soldiers were treated there.

'Thanks. Gifts exchanged …' refers to the gift of the Indian Memorial Gateway at the southern entrance to the site. It was a thank you to the people of Brighton from 'the Princes and people of India'. An inscription on the gate reads, 'This Gateway is the gift of India in commemoration of her sons who stricken in the Great War were tended in the Pavilion in 1914 and 1915'. The Maharajah of Patiola, Bhupinder Singh, dedicated the gateway on 26 October 1921. The mayor, B.N. Southall, reciprocated with the presentation of a gold key to the maharajah. This was a copy of the original key to the Royal Pavilion. Patiola had provided some 28,000 fighters in the First World War from hundreds of remote Indian villages. Those returning home after treatment in the Pavilion Hospital spread the fame of 'Doctor Brighton'.

The use of the Royal Pavilion as a hospital had continued after the departure of the Indian Army patients. From 1916 to 1920 the facilities were used for rehabilitating limbless British soldiers. Some 6,000 men gained skills for employment in various fields, from engineering to cinematography, and a sign on Queen Mary's Workshop, in the Royal Pavilion grounds reads 'Hope Welcomes All Who Enter Here'.

Inevitably, over this period there had been some adverse effects on the buildings' interiors through alterations, damage and neglect, but the town was compensated for this and a programme of restoration, refurbishment and conservation was put in hand. The restoration work was not without setbacks. In 1975 an arson attack resulted in the closure of the Music Room for eleven years, and in the Great Storm of October 1987 a large stone ball dislodged from a minaret plunged through the ceiling of the Music Room, embedding itself in the re-carpeted floor.

The Music Room, now fully restored, was one of George IV's particular extravagances. It was one of the 'showstoppers' of his artist designers, Frederick Crace and Robert Jones. Jones was something of a specialist in over-the-top chandeliers, such as the one in the Banqueting Room. Hence, as well as the inevitable dragons, there were no less than nine lotus-shaped chandeliers.

As with all the main entertaining rooms, it was built to attract and impress his guests. There were performances of Handel and Italian opera. The composer Gioachini Antonio Rossini (1792–1868) performed here in 1823. By that date he had composed the well-known opera, *The Barber of Seville* (1816). Perhaps *Figaro* put in an appearance in the Music Room?

'Firm favourite' stresses the continuing popularity of the Royal Pavilion with visitors – hundreds of thousands each year, 'tracing footsteps of soldiers, of Emperors, of Kings'.

'Film favourite' refers to the use of the Royal Pavilion in films and TV series. These include the films *Richard III* and *The End of the Affair*, and TV series ranging from *The Hairy Bikers* to *Great Britain's Great War* (presented by Jeremy Paxman). The most popular locations are the Music Room, Banqueting Room and Great Kitchen, as well as the exteriors and Regency gardens.

Finally, returning to the poem title, to recognise Brighton and Hove City Council's historic and continuing commitment to the conservation and restoration of the Royal Pavilion – 'Civic Pride', a quote from James A. Owen's 2006 fantasy novel, *Here, There be Dragons*:

> Sometimes it is not about guarding something of value that is important, but rather, being a valuable guard, so that when that thing comes along that needs guarding, there is no question.

THE TURNING POINT

Ruins now. At peace.
Soundtracks of the past give way
to soundtracks of today.
Prayers and the cries of soldiers at war,
recalled by the audio tour,
replaced by the cries of children at play.

The priory – a martyr's dedication,
the namesake – a London railway station!
Alive in altered images,
windows into a bygone age.
Foundation, domination, dissolution,
desecration, excavation, restoration.

The castle – the Earl's reward,
companion to the Conqueror.
Toy houses huddled at its feet,
everyday lives, everyday dreams.
Tourists now scale the keep
from whence a Prince rode forth.

The battle – the baron's revolt.
Death on the Downs, a town in flames,
the king captured, the prince captured.
A battle won, but not the war.
Escape, the king's revenge.
Outnumbered, trapped, slaughtered, crushed.
De Montfort's death. *'Our bodies theirs'.*

But ideas whose time has come live on.
Life, Liberty and the Rule of Law,
Parliament. The turning point.
Democracy his legacy.

7

THE PRIORY OF ST PANCRAS & LEWES CASTLE
SITES THAT PLAYED A PART IN THE BATTLE OF LEWES

Both sites played a part in the Battle of Lewes, 14 May 1264, a turning point in British history. Baroness Andrews, chair of English Heritage and patron of the Battle of Lewes Project, in her opening address to the Battle of Lewes Conference on 14 April 2012, encapsulated this view:

> The popular story of the Battle of Lewes has been told and re-told but there are many unanswered questions ... What we do know is that the battle did open the way for what eventually became a representative democracy. The battlefield at Lewes marks that point when the world turned in a different direction.

Both the priory and the castle are 'Ruins now. At peace.' The 'soundtracks of the past' would have ranged from the prayers and Latin chants of the monks in more peaceful times to the clamour of the Battle of Lewes, as retreating king's soldiers were hotly pursued by those of the victorious Simon de Montfort. From the Downs, north of the town, in the afternoon the fighting descended past the castle, through the streets and into the priory grounds. The cries of the townsfolk and the crackle of burning thatched roofs would have provided the backing track.

The 'soundtracks of today' include an audio tour of the priory grounds by Dr Tony Freedman, linked to the excellent interpretation panels – 'windows into a bygone age'. A particular feature of the panels are the 'altered images'. At each location the image on the panel of the present-day ruined fragments that you see has been extended with the ghostly outlines of the buildings at their most impressive, before the Dissolution of the Monasteries. This really takes you back in time. 'The cries of children at play' is included as a contrast to 'the cries of soldiers at war'. The site is popular with teachers for educational visits as well as for family days out.

The last two lines of Verse 2 compress over 900 years of the history of the priory into six words. This needs quite a bit of explanation. Firstly, though, the priory's dedication to St Pancras.

Pancras of Rome was an early fourth-century martyr, beheaded on 12 May AD 303 for his faith, at the age of 14. This day is celebrated each year as his saint's day. Among other attributions he is a patron saint of children. Six ancient churches in England were dedicated to Pancras, including St Pancras Old

Church in Somerstown, Camden, London NW1. This church is believed to be on one of the oldest sites of Christian worship in England (fourth century). St Augustine is said to have brought some of St Pancras' relics to England, possibly in the sixth century. The dedication is also the explanation for the name of the nearby St Pancras Railway Station.

St Pancras Old Church also has two other rather convoluted links with Sussex. The churchyard contains a memorial tomb for Mary Wollstonecraft (1759–97), philosopher, writer and advocate of women's rights. It was over her tomb that Mary's daughter (also Mary) and the Sussex poet, Percy Bysshe Shelley, planned their 1814 elopement. Mary Shelley, as she became, was also a writer, famous for her novel *Frankenstein*.

The second connection is one of 'desecration' (Verse 2, last line). Both sites were cut through by the building of railway lines in the mid-1800s. In the case of Lewes Priory in 1845, this revealed a mass burial pit containing hundreds of bodies from the Battle of Lewes and, separately, two lead caskets containing the bones of William de Warenne and his wife, founders of both the priory and Lewes Castle.

In the case of St Pancras Old Churchyard, to make way for the railway many bodies had to be exhumed and moved. On this site, though, there was also the problem of the headstones. It was decided to re-erect them around the base of a nearby tree, under the direction of a young local surveyor, later to turn author, Thomas Hardy.

As mentioned above, the 'foundation' of the priory, between 1078 and 1082, was down to the Norman Baron William de Warenne and his wife Gundrada. The priory was built on the site, below Warenne's castle, of an earlier wooden Saxon church. The builders were the first prior, Lanzo, who came over from Cluny (France) with three monks. It was the first Cluniac monastery in England, and over the centuries developed into one of the wealthiest monasteries in the country, accommodating an estimated sixty monks at its peak. The ornately decorated Great Church dominating the almost 40-acre site was longer than Chichester Cathedral, at 420ft, with a roof height of 93–105ft.

The Dissolution of the Monasteries, directed by Thomas Cromwell on the orders of Henry VIII, spelt the end for Lewes Priory. On 16 November 1537, the priory, all its buildings and lands were surrendered by the prior, Robert Crowham, to Thomas Cromwell. He had no choice. A specialist demolition team, led by an Italian engineer Giovanni Portinari, took over the site. They were exceptionally thorough. Sadly, nothing of the Great Church now remains above ground, and only fragments of the other, once extensive, priory buildings.

'Excavation' by archaeologists was initially triggered by the 1845 construction of the Lewes to Brighton railway line through the site and has continued at intervals to the present day. Although a popular visitor attraction in the nineteenth and early twentieth centuries, in recent years, due to a lack of investment, the site had become neglected.

'Restoration' was largely due to the initiative and energy of Dr John Lawrence MBE, president (then chairman) of the Lewes Priory Trust. Funding was won from the Heritage Lottery Fund (£545,000) and English Heritage (£95,000), which with matching funding provided a pot of over £809,000. The planned restoration work was completed on 26 November 2010. Priory Park today is a tribute to the trust's initial faith and ongoing support. Lewes Priory is now a grade one listed building.

Verse 3 now focuses on Lewes Castle, built in 1069, and also the work of William de Warenne. Created 1st Earl of Surrey, he was a companion of William the Conqueror at the Battle of Hastings three years earlier. Built on the highest point of the town, it actually stands on an artificial mound of chalk blocks. An initial wooden keep was replaced by stone.

The castle has perhaps become best known as the stronghold from whence Prince Edward ('Edward Longshanks'), later King Edward I, rode forth with his cavalry to join up with his father King Henry III to join battle with Simon de Montfort's rebel forces in the Battle of Lewes. The king had made the Priory of St Pancras, at the foot of the hill, his headquarters. He had arrived with a large force of infantry on 12 May, the eve of the feast of St Pancras, causing much disruption for the monks.

The Warennes occupied the castle until 1347, when John, the 7th Earl, died without issue. John was buried in Lewes Priory and the title passed to his nephew Richard Fitzalan who was also Earl of Arundel. The castle was leased by the Sussex Archaeological Society ('Sussex Past') from 1850.

The line 'Toy houses huddled at its feet' owes its origin to a remark by William Morris – artist, designer, poet and social reformer. In the winter of 1882, during a stay in the Burne-Joneses' house in Rottingdean, Morris took a long drive with his epileptic daughter Jenny across the Downs. From the top of the hill above Falmer they saw Lewes, 'lying like a box of toys under a great amphitheatre of chalk hills'. The castle was gifted to the Sussex Archaeological Society by Sir Charles Stanford in 1922 and the same experience is now available to all castle visitors without jumping in the car. A realistic scale model, looking down upon the town, can be viewed within the Barbican House Museum.

And so to the Battle of Lewes. When the 9-year-old Henry III became king in 1216, and for the next ten years, England was ruled by a regency. At first this was acceptable to the English barons who were regularly consulted. However, once he began ruling in his own right, increasingly the offices of state came to be occupied by foreign intruders. This was partly the consequence of the monarchy's (lost) French domains and partly due to Henry's marriage to Eleanor of Provence. The barons were not happy. It was relatively few years since the barons' hard-fought battle of wills with King John for acceptance of their 'Articles of the Barons' (now famously known as Magna Carta, of 1215). Henry was not sticking to these principles and so the barons attempted to reduce Henry to the status of a constitutional monarch through the 'Provisions of Oxford' (1258) and 'Provisions of Westminster' (1259).

In these negotiations, the earls and barons were represented by Simon de Montfort. In *A History of the English-Speaking Peoples*, Winston Churchill describes Simon de Montfort as 'the brain and driving force of the English aristocracy'. De Montfort believed that through the council – the Parliament – the king could be controlled. He was wrong. The king and his son, Prince Edward, were not having any of this. What became known as 'the Barons' Revolt' came to a head with the Battle of Lewes on 14 May 1264.

'Death on the Downs' refers to the extreme violence of the morning battle. The previous night, Simon de Montfort's rebel army had marched quietly uphill from Warningore Wood, north-west of the town, and along the ridge from Blackcap to Mount Harry. They had the advantage of the high ground. Just after dawn King Henry III's army (about 10,000 strong) struggled up Winterbourne Hollow and took up positions facing de Montfort's army (about 5,000 strong). The battle is thought to have raged over roughly the area of Lewes Prison, the old racecourse and Landport Bottom.

Despite being heavily outnumbered, due to his greater experience and superior tactics, coupled with a catastrophic mistake on the king's side, Simon de Montfort won the day. In the afternoon the king's troops staged a fighting retreat through the town, through what is now Lewes High Street and School Hill. The remaining castle garrison vainly tried to disrupt the rebel army's pursuit by firing flaming arrows into the thatched roofs of the houses below – 'a town in flames'.

There was no sanctuary in the priory and with many of his supporters having fled, there was no option for the king but to concede defeat. The king was forced to sign a document accepting the 'Provisions of Oxford'. This was called the 'Mise of Lewes'. Prince Edward was held hostage.

There was rejoicing in the country on several levels. The *Song of Lewes*, written in Latin and running to nearly 1,000 lines, was aimed at the educated classes. There is a translated extract encircling the Battle of Lewes memorial in Priory Park. It was optimistic about the king sticking to the 'Mise of Lewes' agreement:

> Now Englishmen, read on about this battle fought at Lewes' walls. Because of this you are alive and safe. Rejoice then in God. Law is like fire, for it lights as truth, warms as charity, burns as zeal. With these virtues as his guides, the King will rule well.
>
>   (Translated extract from the *Song of Lewes*,
>   as on the Battle of Lewes memorial in Priory Park.)

A more scurrilous account, popular with the commoners, was *The Song of the Battle of Lewes*, a poem written in Middle English and now preserved in the British Library. It particularly delights in mocking the king's despised brother, Richard Earl of Cornwall and 'Kyng of Alemaigne' (King of the Germans). Unable to reach the priory, Richard was discovered hiding in a windmill where he was said to have been taunted by rebel soldiers – 'Come down, come down, thou wicked miller!'

The rejoicing didn't last. This was a classic example of 'A battle won, but not the war'. The barons fell out among themselves, Prince Edward escaped, raised an army, and in the 'away match' defeated and killed Simon de Montfort.

The particularly swift and bloody Battle of Evesham (Worcestershire) took place on 4 August 1265. Trapped by overwhelming forces in a loop of the River Avon, Simon is reported to have said, 'God have mercy on our souls, for our bodies are theirs'. The Barons' Revolt had been ruthlessly crushed.

However, this was not the end, but the start of the far more significant story. Once the king could again choose his own holders of office he embraced the principles of Magna Carta, the only respected blueprint for democratic reform, and held regular parliaments.

The irony is that Simon's old adversary, the person responsible for his death, once crowned King Edward I upon the death of his father, consolidated these reforms. For English historians, Edward I's reign is often regarded as the high point of medieval kingship. Simon had died a hero, not only on the battlefield but for his legacy – democracy ('Life, Liberty and the Rule of Law ... ideas whose time has come live on'), 'the turning point'.

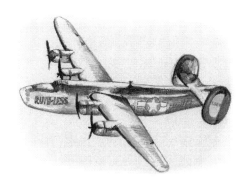

LIBERATOR

Flak knocked out engine 3
Flak crippled engine 4
'Come on Ruth, go girl, we can make it'
'Too low for chrissake!
Too low, get her up, get her up'.
Too low ...
***
Remembrance. Fifty years of trudging up a hillside,
flowers at the spot. Arthur never forgot.
Today,
comrades, relatives, veterans,
a bugler (Last Post), Standards proudly raised,
then dipped. Arthur removed
the blood-stained folded hat,
rolled back the Stars and Stripes.
'OUR FRIENDS AND ALLIES
FAR FROM HOME'
Arkansas, Alabama, New York, South Carolina,
Tennessee, South Dakota, Massachusetts, Pennsylvania.
***
Remembered. Each year,
echoes, tears, pride, elation, celebrations.
Hurricane, Spitfire, Lancaster – comrades in arms,
Vulcan, Cold War warriors – inheritors,
Tornado, Typhoon – new kids on the block,
Low, but not too low, not
Too low ...
***
Today, new scars across a blood-red sky.
Today, high over Beachy Head,
but a world away. Memories, reveries,
gently interrupted.
'What's our plane, Daddy?'
'747'
'What was Grandad's plane, Daddy?'
'Liberator, Amy,
Too low ...'

8

THE LIBERATOR MEMORIAL

THE CRASH SITE OF A US AIR FORCE SECOND WORLD WAR BOMBER, NEAR BEACHY HEAD

This is not about a 'famous' Sussex place. It is unlikely to be known to many readers other than those who keep alive memories of significant local events during the Second World War.

The Liberator Memorial is off the beaten track, both physically and compared to the better-known local memorial to RAF Bomber Command at Beachy Head. Those who come across it while exploring the hillside around Butts Brow (OS grid reference TQ579017) inevitably find this simple memorial deeply moving.

By their very nature some Second World War air crash memorials are in infrequently visited places. The Liberator Memorial, however, occupies a stunning position on the top of the Downs looking out over Eastbourne towards the sea. It is also significant in being a memorial to a US Air Force bomber crew who gave their lives fighting alongside us.

The B-24 Liberator bomber, named *Ruth-less* by the pilot after his wife, of necessity left behind, was returning from a daylight raid on a V2 rocket facility at Watten, Pas-de-Calais, on 2 February 1944. Forty nine B-24s had taken part. It was one of many raids on the Watten bunker between 27 August 1943 and 25 August 1944. Up until the last three months the raids were carried out almost exclusively by USAAF B-24 Liberator bombers. The final missions were taken up by RAF Lancasters, Halifaxes and Mosquitos – 'comrades in arms'.

Ruth-less was hit by enemy fire. Number 3 inboard engine was knocked out. Number 4 engine, also hit, was streaming fuel. Liberators were particularly vulnerable to battle damage, particularly fire – they were nicknamed 'flying coffins' by crews. The pilot, First Lieutenant James Bolin, realised that they wouldn't make it back to their base at Shipdham (RAF Shipdham, 3 miles south of Dereham in Norfolk, was the American 8th Air Force heavy bomber base).

He turned towards Beachy Head, aiming for the small grass airfield at Friston. By a cruel twist of fate, another aircraft was landing as he approached and so he had to make a second run. Buffeted by strong winds and in a dense fog he circled Eastbourne almost at rooftop level. It was reported that eyewitnesses in their gardens could see the crew through the windows of the bomber. The Liberators were, at the best of times, difficult to fly, needing heavy control forces. Unable to gain enough height – they were just 30ft too low – *Ruth-less* slammed into the hillside nose first. The aircraft cartwheeled and disintegrated in a ball of fire. All but two of the crew of ten died instantly.

The two survivors were taken to the Princess Alice Hospital in Eastbourne but died within twenty-four hours. The following eyewitness accounts are taken from Chapter 8, 'Hurry Home Boys', *Eighth Air Force Bomber Stories*, and quoted on page 205 of the 44th Bomb Group Roll of Honor:

> ... the bomber appeared, flying slowly and looking exhausted according to Mrs. Barrow. She saw an airman standing at one of the waist-gun windows, and her heart went out to him. As it went by she whispered: 'Hurry home, boys'.
> A schoolboy, Derek Wilkinson, was outside on the grass at Willingdon Golf Course. He saw the bomber and realized that unless it gained altitude it would crash into the nearby hills. On those hills was Audrey Armstrong, rounding up sheep with the golf-club's greenskeeper. She heard the straining engines and saw the pilot as both realized that a crash was inevitable. The aircraft crashed into the hill and exploded. An engine tumbled down the hill near her. She and the greenskeeper ran toward the wreck once the explosions had stopped, but found only smouldering debris. Amazingly there were some signs of life. One aviator died at the scene despite receiving first aid. Two more died later at a nearby hospital.

The objective of the many raids, to prevent the V2 rocket facility at Watten becoming operational, was achieved, although the massive concrete bunker survived. Now known as *Le Blockhaus d'Éperlecques*, and designated a *monument historique* and open to the public, it is part of a museum recording the history of the German V-weapons programme.

Fifty years after the crash in 1994, two local men, Kevin Watson and George Dixon, approached Eastbourne Borough Council with regard to placing a permanent memorial at the crash site. The *Ruth-less* Memorial Fund commissioned the rectangular memorial of Norwegian granite set horizontally on a low concrete plinth. The polished and raised lettering underneath a carved relief image of the bomber reads:

In memory of the crew of a B-24D Liberator Bomber
N° 41-24282 BAR Y 'RUTH-LESS'
of
506 Squadron, 44th Bombardment Group, 8th U.S.A.F.
who all lost their lives, when,
badly damaged by enemy action and in very low cloud,
the aircraft crashed here on February 2nd 1944.

[*The carved names and home towns and states of the ten crew members are then listed.*]

OUR FRIENDS AND ALLIES
FAR FROM HOME

On Saturday, 13 May 1995 a service was held to unveil and consecrate the memorial. It was an outstanding act of remembrance. At least 400 people attended. These included relatives of the dead airmen; serving and veteran USAAF officers; the band, standard bearers and members of the Royal British Legion; the boys and girls of the local Air Training Corps; the local Member of Parliament, Nigel Waterson; councillors and officials.

There was a Stars and Stripes made of flowers, among other memorial wreaths. The band preceded the playing of the American national anthem during the ceremony with 'Old Folks at Home' as the gathering assembled. It was an ecumenical service with three ministers participating. The American Ambassador was represented by Lieutenant Colonel Snukis of the US Marines, who made a speech reminding the assembly of past sacrifices made so that we can be free today.

For Arthur King, after 'fifty years of trudging up a hillside, flowers at the spot', this was his time to step forward. 'Arthur never forgot' – every Remembrance Sunday for fifty years, whatever the weather, he had trudged up the steep incline to lay flowers at the very spot where the Liberator had crashed, up until now otherwise unmarked. He recounted that his wife used to say to him, 'You must be bloody mad!'

The monument had been covered with the American flag. Also, resting in the centre was 'the blood-stained folded hat' of First Lieutenant Orville Wulff, which had been found in his breast pocket when he died. Arthur was called forward to remove the hat and roll back the Stars and Stripes. Up until then, although a bit breezy the weather had been kind, but at that very moment a few large raindrops started to fall – 'teardrops from heaven', as one of those attending later remarked. A bugler sounded the last post, Standards were dipped and, right on cue, the RAF's Red Arrows display team roared overhead, dipping their wings in salute. (The Red Arrows have been displaying since 1965, initially in Folland Gnats, but since 1979 in BAE Systems Hawk T1s. It is possible to request a fly-past when the Red Arrows are already going to be in transit nearby. The year of the memorial dedication, 1995, was the year in which they performed their greatest number of displays – 136 appearances, including the start of a world tour from October 1995 to February 1996.)

Each year now, on Remembrance Day in November, a service is held at the Liberator Memorial. A group also visits each May. A video of the 2007 Remembrance Day service also recorded a tribute to the pilots of two Spitfires who, it was revealed, had also crashed on this same hillside, but to whom there is no physical memorial.

Each year the RAF Red Arrows return to thrill the crowds at Airbourne (Eastbourne's International Airshow). The mainly military aircraft line-up showcases both the 'comrades in arms' of the Liberator and the succeeding generations. The heavy bomber role in the Second World War was shared with the Avro Lancaster which, together with the Supermarine Spitfire and the Hawker Hurricane, now make up the Battle of Britain Memorial Flight (BBMF).

The 'Cold War warrior', inheritor of the role of the heavy bombers, was the Vulcan. This came from the same stable as the Lancaster (Avro). This jet-powered delta-wing strategic bomber served with the RAF from 1956 until 1984. It was the most technically advanced of the three V-bombers. The others were the Handley Page Victor (later to be used as the Vulcan's air-to-air refuelling tanker on the Falklands mission) and the Vickers Valiant. The Vulcan represented the peak of technical development of the long-range heavy bomber concept during the Cold War. This period of political and military tension between the powers of the Western Bloc (the USA, its NATO allies and others) and powers in the Eastern Bloc (the Soviet Union and its allies in the Warsaw Pact) saw the Vulcan force armed with Britain's nuclear deterrent. In the James Bond film *Thunderball*, Emilio Largo steals the nuclear weapons from an Avro Vulcan.

The Vulcan was also designed to use conventional bombs. The notable occasion on which this capability was employed was in the bombing of Stanley Airport runway during the Falklands War between the UK and Argentina. In 1992, its operational days over, Avro Vulcan B.2 XH558, *The Spirit of Great Britain*, was retired. It was the last in service with the RAF. A group of enthusiasts were determined that it should not just spend the rest of its days as a static display. Since 2007 the Vulcan to the Sky Trust, with the support of public and corporate donations, has kept this iconic example of British engineering excellence and design flying.

As far as an aircraft can have a personality or star quality, she possessed it. Sadly, following a national 'farewell tour' she flew for the last time in October 2015. A particular highlight of the tour was when the Red Arrows flew with the Vulcan for the final time on 22 September 2015 at the Southport Air Show. The nine Red Arrows formed a V-shape in front of the Vulcan – echoing her V-shaped wing. Lumps in throats! Engineers for the trust were unable to guarantee her airworthiness beyond that date. She is now kept in taxiable condition at Robin Hood Airport, Doncaster.

Moving on to the 'new kids on the block', the Tornado and Typhoon. The Panavia Tornado entered service with the RAF in 1979–80 and is projected to continue until 2025. The Tornado is a multi-role fighter/bomber with a variable sweep wing. A very noisy and somewhat chunky 'kid on the block', its British nickname is 'Tonka' – but what a very dangerous toy! It is perhaps the nearest successor to *Ruth-less*. Although single role, long-range heavy bombers have faded from the scene, the Tornado can carry out precision bombing. This role is now carried out using air-launched missiles or 'smart bombs' though, rather than the 'dumb bombs' of the Second World War. Strategic long-range bombing has been superseded by intercontinental ballistic missiles, often submarine based.

The successor to the Spitfires and Hurricanes of the Second World War is the multi-role Eurofighter Typhoon, which came into service with the RAF in 2007, at air shows the flashiest 'new kid on the block'.

And 'Today, new scars across a blood-red sky' – Amy and her father 'high over Beachy Head'. Their own passenger airliner could well have been the ubiquitous 'jumbo jet', the Boeing 747. As with other veteran's families, this father and daughter may have acted upon the reminder in the Spring 1996 issue of the *44th Bomb Group Veterans Association Journal*, 'The 44th has a standing invitation to visit with the people of Eastbourne, who have for 52 years treated the loss of the "Ruthless" crew as if it were their own sons who perished in the crash'.

Relatives visiting the Liberator Memorial crash site in recent years may well have included grandchildren of the dead airmen.

WEST
SUSSEX

PHOENIX REBORN

Visited before,
Visited after.
Phoenix reborn.
House within house.

Our tour left no legacy,
no highlights adorned our walls.
No loves lost then found,
no scandals.

Harry's loves bookended his life.
His first love lost,
less than a year and she was gone,
no lady then,
a lady later.
Another's victory.

Time passed
Scents of summers
Changing seasons
Changing views.

And then,
his last love found.
But a maid,
separated by years
but united by song.
Fellow travellers
to the ends of time,
together.

9

UPPARK HOUSE AND GARDEN
RESTORED FROM THE
ASHES OF A DEVASTATING FIRE

The building of Uppark House was first started in 1690, but it is usually referred to as an eighteenth-century house. On 30 August 1989 it suffered a major fire, caused by a workman's blowtorch while repairing lead flashing on the roof. The National Trust, despite the cost and at least one dissenting Member of Parliament, with the agreement of their insurers decided to rebuild and restore this important house to the state it was in the days before the fire. In fact, the £20 million restoration cost was a cheaper insurance settlement than the pay-out for a complete loss. The house was reopened in 1995 – 'a near seamless mix of old and new'. (The 'phoenix reborn', in Greek mythology, is a long-lived bird that is cyclically reborn. It dies in flames and is reborn from the ashes.)

'House within house' refers not only to the original house within the parts restored, but also to the important eighteenth-century Palladian-style doll's house (1735–40) within.

Uppark was purchased in 1747 by Sir Matthew Fetherstonhaugh. Sir Matthew and his wife, Lady Sarah, undertook the fashionable Grand Tour shortly after (1749–52), resulting in the acquisition of the nucleus of the collection of eighteenth-century Italian paintings in the house. A highlight of their tour was having their portraits painted in Rome, by the international 'star' Pompeo Batoni (1708–87). The clue here were the lines 'Our tour left no legacy, no highlights adorned our walls', contrasting current holiday tours to that of the Fetherstonhaughs' Grand Tour.

When Sir Matthew died in 1774, Uppark passed to his son, Sir Harry Fetherstonhaugh (1754–1846), a great friend of the Prince Regent. Perhaps in competition with his friend, Harry added to the treasures.

Harry's love life raised more than a few eyebrows though. His first love, born Emma Lyon, was a teenage London night club hostess, a Cheshire girl. They met in 1780, when Harry was 26, and he brought her back to Uppark. However, within a year she was sent back to London, six months' pregnant, and in the course of another romantic attachment she changed her name to Emma Hart. Rejected once again, but nothing deterred, in 1791 she married well to Sir William Hamilton. Two years later, now Lady Emma Hamilton, she first met a rising star naval officer. They were soulmates. Emma and Admiral Lord Nelson's lifelong love affair has of course become legend. On a fine day, from Uppark you can see the Spinnaker Tower in Portsmouth, final resting place of Nelson's most famous ship, HMS *Victory*.

Sir Harry, 'His first love lost', threw himself into remodelling the house and gardens. In 1810, Humphrey Repton, the successor to Capability Brown, remarked on the 'olfactory joy' the gardens provided. The overwhelming scent at that time would probably have been from Heliotrope, commonly known as 'Cherry Pie'.

Sir Harry's 'last love found', at the age of 71, was the 20-year-old Mary Ann. Without wife and children, one day walking past the dairy he heard her singing. He walked into the dairy and proposed to his dairy maid. They married in 1825 and were a devoted couple until he died in 1846, aged 92.

Writing in 1855 in his book *Popular Music of the Olden Time*, the acknowledged authority, William Chappell, conjectured:

> If I were required to name three of the most popular songs among the servant-maids of the present generation, I should say, from my own experience, that they are 'Cupid's Garden', 'I sow'd the seeds of love' and 'Early one morning'.

The lyrics of 'Early One Morning' can be dated back to 1787 – a broadside in the Bodleian Library, Oxford, dates from about 1803. It is entirely possible that this was one of the songs that Sir Harry heard Mary Ann singing that morning:

> Early one morning, just as the sun was rising
> I heard a maid sing in the valley below
> 'Oh don't deceive me, Oh never leave me,
> How could you use, a poor maiden so?'
> (Verse 1 of seven – there are many variations on the lyrics.)

'Fellow travellers to the ends of time ...' refers not only to the couple's devotion, but also to another famous occupant. H.G. Wells spent part of his boyhood at Uppark. His mother, Sarah, was employed as housekeeper and his father, Joseph, as a gardener. His experiences at Uppark may have influenced his novel *The Time Machine*. The many underground tunnels of the house reappear as the underground passages of the novel. The two fictional races of the novel, encountered 800,000 years in the future, the Eloi (above ground), passive, gentle, but indolent, may be an evolutionary dig at the aristocracy (above stairs), whereas the light-hating Morlocks (below ground) perhaps equate to the servants (below stairs):

> The Upper-world people might once have been the favoured aristocracy, and the Morlocks their mechanical servants: but that had long since passed away. ... The Eloi, like the Carolingian kings, had decayed to a more beautiful futility. They still possessed the earth on sufferance, since the Morlocks, subterranean for innumerable generations, had come at last to find the daylit surface intolerable.

The servants' working areas in the basement at Uppark, notably the kitchen, are still as they were when the young H.G. Wells was exploring the house.

RESCUED

Museum. The roof the sky, the woods, the walls.
Six centuries, but more than memories,
survivors – relocated, resurrected, cherished.
Wood and plaster, brick and stone.

Bayleaf, boarhunt, bellframe, barn,
tollhouse, tabernacle, forge,
sawpit, granary, windpump, whim,
cattle-shed, wagon-shed, farm.

Assembled to inspire, delight.
Faded echoes, silent tears,
peals of laughter, misplaced fears –
our half-term hosts the friendly ghosts.

Thatcher, tanner, tiler,
miller, mason, smith,
carver, weaver, dauber,
yeoman, squatter, serf.

Women spun and sewed and wove,
menfolk fashioned tools,
women cooked and cleaned, conceived,
a swelling nest of mouths
the husband's wage to feed,
'He is bailiff, woodman, wheelwright, field surveyor, engineer,
and if flagrantly a poacher, – 'tain't for me to interfere.'

Times past, times present.
Down the lane, one hundred years
For Home and Country.
Old skills, new skills,
inspiring women, nationwide.

In the rain, two hundred years,
soaked on a Rural Ride.
Dancing, singing, food and folk,
heavy horses pull the plough,
gilded horses thrill the fair.
Time travellers, filmed and feted, celebrated.

10

WEALD AND DOWNLAND OPEN AIR MUSEUM
RESCUED HISTORIC BUILDINGS

A wider recognition is necessary of the extent of England's heritage in her old cottages and the sturdy country stock that dwell in them. For both heritages are wasting and in jeopardy; the cottages are being destroyed, the folk leaving the country. It is for England to foster, cherish, and preserve them both. If she is unworthy, they will both, to her permanent detriment, largely vanish from the face of the land. (Harry Batsford and Charles Fry, *The English Cottage*, first published in October 1938.)

In response to such concerns, the Weald & Downland Open Air Museum was launched in 1967 by a small group of enthusiasts led by the museum's founder, the late Dr J.R. Armstrong MBE. It opened to the public on 4 September 1970.

The museum, a registered charity, has done more than just rescue 'cottages'. Where it has not been possible to retain buildings on their original sites, a representative selection of historic buildings of all types have been 'relocated, resurrected, cherished'. These illustrate the developments in rural building styles and types, 'wood and plaster, brick and stone', over the last six centuries. The site covers some 40 acres. A few of the fifty different buildings' given names and types have been fashioned into the chant-like second verse.

The reasons for their relocation include making way for the Eurotunnel terminal, a new housing estate, a new reservoir, road widening and sand quarrying. The earliest structure in the museum, the thirteenth-century Hangleton Cottage, was even reconstructed from excavated evidence on the site of a village lost during the Black Death. Simon Jenkins, in *England's Thousand Best Houses*, recognises 'its like' – 'It is the simplest possible dwelling, standard throughout England for over a thousand years. I have seen its like from the Amazon to the Himalayas.'

The 'youngest' reconstructed cottages (Whitaker's Cottages), a pair of tiny semi-detached cottages, were built for rent in the 1860s. They were saved from being demolished to make way for a housing estate and re-erected at the museum in 1987. Six centuries on from Hangleton Cottage though, the worker's cottage was still a basic affair. A Board of Agriculture report in 1796 proposed that 'twelve feet is a width sufficient for a dwelling that is deemed to be a cottage; if it be wider it approaches too near to what I would call a house for a superior tradesman'.

The planning recommendations at the time that Whitaker's Cottages were constructed, some seventy years on, although still conforming to the 12ft width, did sound more considerate – if a bit patronising. The recommendations are set out in *An Encyclopaedia of Architecture* by J. Gwilt, published in 1876:

No cottage ought to be erected which does not contain a warm, comfortable plain room, with an oven to bake the bread of its occupier, a small closet for the beer and provisions, two wholesome lodging rooms, one whereof should be for the man and his wife, and the other for his children.

This was in fact the classic 'two up, two down'. Regarding the heritage of 'the sturdy country stock that dwell in them', the museum preserves and promotes their traditional craft skills. This is achieved through exhibitions, courses, workshops, living history demonstrations, an extensive calendar of special events, provision for visiting school parties, and displays and collections of tools and artefacts in the Building Crafts Gallery and the multi-award-winning Downland Gridshell building (2002).

The chant like fourth verse celebrates the craft heritage of these people. The meaning of the term 'squatters' has changed over time. Squatters originally referred to smallholders who either owned land freehold, which they had originally cleared (from forests), or else had maintained their hereditary village holdings.

Verse 5 gives an insight into day-to-day cottage life in the sixteenth and seventeenth centuries, as graphically described by Lord Ernle in his *English Farm, Past and Present*, and quoted in the Batsford book, *The English Cottage*. The 'swelling nest of mouths the husband's wage to feed' identifies the cottager's chief burden since the Middle Ages, the unwieldy size of his ever-increasing family. These lines are an interpretation of a passage from *Piers Plowman*, written at the time (the late fourteenth century) in the language of the time (Middle English) and attributed to William Langland. Langland lived at the same time as the better-known Geoffrey Chaucer, author of *The Canterbury Tales*. They were both keen observers of the society they lived in.

The last two lines of this verse are borrowed from Rudyard Kipling's poem 'The Land', in his collection, *A Diversity of Creatures*. Kipling was one of a roll-call of influential champions of the field workers and master craftsmen who he claimed to be the real owners of the English country.

'Assembled to inspire, delight ... half-term hosts the friendly ghosts' (Verse 3) illustrates one of the fun ways in which the museum encourages schoolchildren to connect with the buildings and their occupants. The verse highlights a common belief about old houses, namely that they may be haunted. These rescued houses are no different. In particular, the very atmospheric Pendean Farmhouse (1609), furnished with replica items, has the reputation of having a resident ghost. The theme was taken further in two forty-four minute TV programmes, *Most Haunted: Weald and Downland*.

The last two verses pick out two anniversaries in 2015 which the museum celebrated with special events. The first was the centenary of the Women's Institute (WI). Founded in Canada in 1897, it was started in Britain in 1915 with the aim of encouraging countrywomen to help increase the food supply to a war-torn nation. Singleton and East Dean WI, 'down the lane', was the first branch to be formed in England. 'For Home and Country' was the WI's first motto, and 'Inspiring women for 100 years' is their current motto, devised for the centenary year. 'Old skills, new skills' emphasises the fact that the WI is now much more than 'Jam and Jerusalem'. While preserving and passing on old skills, their extensive education programme provides the chance to build new skills and to campaign for contemporary causes.

The second anniversary of the museum, which took place on the exact date, was marked by a 4-mile guided walk, following in the hoof prints of one of William Cobbett's *Rural Rides*, which passed through East Dean to Singleton on 2 August 1823. He should have enjoyed far-reaching views, particularly from the summit of Duncton Down, an OS map viewpoint, 'But, alas! Saint Swithin had begun his work for the day'. When he arrived in Singleton, he wrote in his journal:

> This is really a soaking day, thus far. I got here at nine o'clock (for breakfast). I stripped off my coat, and put it by the kitchen fire. In a parlour just eight feet square, I have another fire, and have dried my shirt on my back. We shall see what this does for a hooping cough.

It is to be hoped that the weather was kinder for the anniversary walkers.

A few of the regular events from the museum's calendar are the subjects of the last lines – 'Dancing, singing' (the December tree dressing), 'Food and folk' (the May festival of this name, with more music and dancing), 'Heavy horses pull the plough' (the October Autumn Countryside Show), and 'gilded horses thrill the fair' (the August Vintage & Steam Festival, including the popular steam-powered carousel gallopers, a beautifully restored roundabout).

The final line, 'Time travellers, filmed and feted, celebrated', acknowledges the museum's appeal for filmmakers. The museum website lists eighteen past productions (with attributions) in the last seven years alone. The production *The Time Travellers Guide to the Elizabethans* was that referred to in the poem line. Others have included *Escape to the Country, Tudor Monastery Farm, Flog it!, Hairy Bikers, Celebrity Antiques Roadtrip* and parts of Shakespeare's *Henry VI* – a truly wide-ranging mix!

To end as we started, with the primary aim of the Weald and Downland Museum, 'to preserve and generate an increased public awareness and interest in the built environment, and specifically historic rural buildings', a collection of quotations:

> I have always felt that the best security for civilisation is the dwelling, and that upon properly appointed and becoming dwellings depends more than anything else the improvement of mankind. Such dwellings are the nursery of all domestic virtues, and without a becoming home the exercise of these virtues is impossible.
>
> (Benjamin Disraeli, prime minister of the UK, 1868, 1874–80.)

The 'becoming home', the 'security' for the individual, and thus 'for civilisa-tion' is a theme clearly illustrated by those suffering from homesickness when abroad, when at war or when under stress. This is a theme running through literature, from Ovid (43 BC–AD 17) when exiled from Rome to the Black Sea by the Emperor Augustus; through Robert Browning (1812–89), having eloped to Italy with Elizabeth Barrett, his wife to be, 'Oh, to be in England, Now that April's there …' (the opening lines of his poem, *Home – Thoughts, From Abroad*); to Robert Frost (1874–1963) and of course the poets of the Great War.

Marcus Tullius Cicero, elected consul of the Roman Empire by the Senate for the year 63 BC, during a stressful time, knew where he'd rather be, 'There is no place more delightful than one's own fireside'. Unfortunately, this wasn't to last. He was subsequently executed upon the orders of Mark Antony.

George Washington, first President of the United States of America (1789–97), shared the same sentiment, but in his case did survive to enjoy it, 'I had rather be on my farm than be Emperor of the world'.

Finally, as Channing Pollock (1880–1946), American playwright and critic, put it, 'Home is the most popular, and will be the most enduring of all earthly establishments'. It is our homes, our houses, that often define us and to which we return. It is just this which the Weald and Downland Open Air Museum has made its mission to preserve. It is more than just a collection of buildings. After all, in the oft-quoted words of an unknown author, 'A house is made of walls and beams; a home is built with love and dreams'.

THAT HOUSE OF ART

From border castle to Sussex mansion,
forced south by a cautious queen.
Four hundred years
and still under a father's watchful eye.

Inside,
below stairs, in new hands,
old traditions,
in Mrs Brown's kitchens.
Above stairs, in ancient hand,
a different cook's tale.

Outside,
her namesake reclaimed past lands.
Parterres to pleasure grounds,
perfected nature.

Beyond,
a distant church,
burnished waters under a setting sun,
sounds of leather on willow,
of clashing antlers,
frozen in time by the painter of light,
another window for that house of art.

11

PETWORTH HOUSE AND PARK
A HISTORIC HOUSE WITH AN OUTSTANDING ART COLLECTION

Petworth House, one of the Percy family's earliest possessions, became their permanent home in the late 1500s after Queen Elizabeth I confined them to the south of England. They were forced to leave their northern estates as Elizabeth I suspected they may have been in league with her rival, Mary, Queen of Scots. Henry Percy, 1st Earl of Northumberland, had inherited Egremont Castle and estates in 1369, and his successors have kept the Lord Egremont title to the present day.

Petworth House and park was handed over to the National Trust in 1947. For the past 250 years it had been in the hands, by inheritance, of the Wyndham family. The current Lord and Lady Egremont still live in the South Wing, still under the 'watchful eye' of the portrait of Elizabeth I's father, Henry VIII (1491–1547). The portrait, by an unknown artist in the style of Hans Holbein (1497/8–1543), may well have been painted in Henry's lifetime or soon after his death. It is now in the main section of the house open to the public, in the Carved Room, so named because of the outstanding wood carvings by Grinling Gibbons and his associates. These include the portrait's elaborate frame, added some time after 1690 during the construction of the original room. The room you see today is a result of the remodelling and doubling in size by the 3rd Earl about 100 years later.

Below stairs, the kitchen still contains the 'Batterie de cuisine', over 1,000 copper saucepans and other utensils which would have been in use in the days when the house and park was tended by about forty live-in servants. 'Mrs Brown's Kitchen' is the name of the National Trust event weekends demonstrating the cooking of traditional recipes, but thankfully not resulting in the cleaning of all that copper!

Above stairs, in the Somerset Room, is a 1410 handwritten copy of Geoffrey Chaucer's *Canterbury Tales* ('The Leconfield Chaucer'), one of which is 'The Cook's Tale'.

Outside, the park, originally the site of the medieval village of Tillington, has undergone a series of transformations down the centuries. In 2013 an 'Archaeology of the Park' project saw over 100 volunteer assistant archaeologists digging into the past 800 years of the life of the grounds, including searching for the site of a banqueting house built by Henry VIII during the time that he owned the park and in use in the sixteenth century. In the succeeding centuries the grounds first became vast formal gardens, a particular feature of which were the parterres, before a 'natural' look was reinstated by Lancelot 'Capability' Brown in the 1750s. He landscaped the existing 700-acre deer park, complete with Doric temple, and created the 'Pleasure Grounds', a 30-acre woodland garden.

The present late seventeenth-century mansion was inherited in 1765 by the art-loving 3rd Earl of Egremont, and so began a golden age. A keen collector and patron, he was host to many contemporary painters and sculptors, giving them the facilities for working in the house and grounds. Both J.M.W. Turner (1775–1851) and John Constable (1776–1837), at separate times, used the old library as a studio. The earl commissioned Turner to paint scenes at or near Petworth as groups of panels for the dining room. The artist produced two sets of paintings, one of which is still in the house; the other is now in Room 102 in the Clore Gallery at the Tate Gallery in London. The last verse of the poem refers to two of these pictures, *Petworth Park: Tillington Church in the distance* (*c.* 1828) and *The Lake, Petworth: Sunset, Fighting Bucks.* The latter shows a cricket match and stags fighting.

As Rebecca Rose relates in her article 'Turner at Petworth', Turner liked to get away from the smoke of London, fishing in the lake and going for walks in the park, often setting out at sunset. Because of his skill in capturing light effects right across his range of classical, landscape and maritime subjects, he became known as 'the painter of light'.

Turner broke with artistic convention. He was a painter of the Romantic period, towards the end of his life taking landscape painting to the limits of Romanticism. From the 1840s, when in his late 60s, to his death in 1851 at the age of 76, his highly atmospheric paintings foreshadowed Impressionism and his spontaneity the approach of some modern abstract artists. Few people understood this work during his lifetime. The Petworth Collection, though, was mainly painted between 1827 and 1837, before this later period.

The 3rd Earl of Egremont also broke with convention as a 'hands-on' patron and collector. He admired Turner's vision. Turner came to stay each year for about a week – with his fishing tackle of course. It was in the nature of a working holiday in the company of fellow artist guests. He much enjoyed the social life, music recitals, table games and fine dining, and documented this in a series of watercolour drawings on blue paper (now mainly in the Turner Bequest at Tate Britain).

Turner's works, however, just added to an existing wide-ranging art collection – what John Constable referred to as 'that house of art' during his two visits in 1834. Constable himself produced around forty watercolours and drawings in and around Petworth. These are now mainly in the V&A and the British Museum in London.

Constable and Turner, however, were chalk and cheese. It took Constable some time to accept an invitation to stay from Lord Egremont, and only then at the urging of his friend and future biographer, Charles Leslie. Leslie was himself a regular visitor to Petworth with his family. In 1824, the earl had seen some of

Constable's work, but the earl's 'constructive criticism' had been taken entirely the wrong way, 'He recollected all my pictures of any note, but he recollected them only for their defects ... The truth is landscape affords him no interest whatever.' (Quoted in *John Constable: A Kingdom of his Own*, Anthony Bailey.) And this about the patron of J.M.W. Turner! Constable could be awkward at times.

Ten years after this reaction though, Constable did accept an invitation to Petworth 'for a few days'. He stayed for two weeks, using a carriage which the earl had put at his disposal for sketching trips in the area. He filled a large sketchbook with drawings and also two watercolours. He was not the social-ite that Turner was, though, always 'full of fun', and was glad to get home. He never returned, and for some reason Lord Egremont never bought a Constable painting.

For both Turner and Constable, as well as many of their contemporaries, the initial draw of 'that house of art' lay in its existing internationally impor-tant art collection. Most of these works are still at Petworth, forming one of the National Trust's finest collections of pictures. Artists represented include Titian, Hieronymus Bosch, Claude Lorrain, Jacob van Ruisdael, David Teniers, Sir Anthony Van Dyke, Sir Peter Lely, Sir Godfrey Kneller, Sir Joshua Reynolds, William Blake and Thomas Gainsborough.

ANCIENT & MODERN

Landmark of faith, landmark for sailors,
a sure foundation, but an unsure foundation,
collapsed, rebuilt, collapsed, rebuilt,
burnt, defaced, plundered,
but a proud survivor.

On foot ...
the people's Saint, lifting their burden,
preaching his cause, crusader in a cassock,
his words his weapons. His shrine still speaks
across the years, St Richard's prayer.

Work of human hands ...
Lazarus lies in stone, awaiting
the resurrection and the life.
'The earl and countess lie in stone',
his hand holding hers, forever,
'What will survive of us is love.'

Work of human hands ...
Paintings, sculpture, tapestry, glass,
bold commissions by a patron dean.
Old settings, new life,
Ancient & Modern.

And music ...
Organ, choirs, the lunchtime concerts, 'Chichester Psalms',
the hint of *West Side Story*.
The popstars in the nave –
'... let everything that hath breath praise the Lord',
but would Gustav turn in his grave?

12

CHICHESTER CATHEDRAL

NOTABLE FOR ITS WORKS OF ART AND ITS MUSICAL TRADITION

Christianity was brought to Sussex by St Wilfred in AD 681 with the building of the first small cathedral, possibly at Church Norton on the coast near Selsey. This was for the South Saxons.

The building of the current cathedral (The Cathedral Church of the Holy Trinity) was started by Bishop Stigand, the first Norman bishop, in 1076 on the site of the Saxon church of St Peter, in Chichester. The change of location came about because the year before, in accordance with Norman policy, the See of the bishop had been moved to a larger centre of population. The poem's opening phrase, 'Landmark of faith', refers to this policy.

The 'landmark for sailors' refers to the later completion of the spire (about 1402), visible across the flat meadows from the sea. 'The spire and countryside form an equation or a symbol experienced by millions of people every year, which cannot be given a value purely in terms of landscape or architecture' (Nikolaus Pevsner, architectural historian).

Building continued for thirty-two years, being completed and consecrated under Bishop Ralph de Luffa in 1108. Stone quarried in the Isle of Wight was used. As was to be discovered later in the course of several rebuildings and extensions, however, the site was prone to subsidence and also the building stone suffered badly from the effects of weathering over the long term.

As indicated in the first verse, over the centuries the cathedral has had a bad time. It has twice been damaged by fire, and at different times both towers have collapsed. The spire had to be repaired by Sir Christopher Wren in the seventeenth century, survived a lightning strike in 1721, but finally telescoped in on itself in 1861. Queen Victoria was among the contributors to the rebuilding fund. Sir George Gilbert Scott carried out the rebuilding over a five-year period. Undaunted, he even made it a few feet taller, but wisely stopped short of matching the height of Salisbury Cathedral's spire. It now stands at 82m.

Because of the subsidence problems, Chichester is the only English cathedral to have a freestanding medieval bell tower. Such campaniles are common in Italy, perhaps the most famous being the Leaning Tower of Pisa – they obviously didn't reckon on subsidence either!

It hasn't just been forces of nature. The cathedral's artefacts were defaced during the Reformation in the sixteenth century, on the orders of King Henry VIII. This included the destruction of St Richard's shrine. Then in 1642 the cathedral's library was plundered by Parliamentary troops. Despite all

these disasters the cathedral is 'a proud survivor'. In fact the architectural histo-rian Nikolaus Pevsner called it 'the most typical English cathedral'. It does make you wonder about some of the others!

Moving on to the next verses, we turn from the building to the people. In the early years, Chichester Cathedral was the See of a celebrated bishop, whose shrine remains a centre of pilgrimage to the present day. Bishop Richard de Wyche (1197–1253) was a hero to his people. The Pope consecrated him Bishop of Chichester in 1245 but due to Church/state politics King Henry III refused to recognise his appointment. He had no income or access to his cathe-dral or diocese for two years, until the king relented. Nothing daunted, during this time he took his ministry to those parts of Sussex to which he did have access, penniless and on foot. He had a frugal diet (he was a strict vegetarian), by choice as well as necessity, and won the hearts of the people. He was the opposite of a 'prince bishop'.

Restored to his cathedral and his income, he continued his frugal lifestyle, concentrating on improving the lot of the people. But he was destined to fulfil a wider role. In 1250, the Crusade in the Holy Land was faltering and the king needed to rally the support of the Church and the people. Bishop Richard was appointed by the Pope to carry out a supportive preaching tour in southern England. It was a punishing schedule and Richard was already 56 years of age and in poor health. Nevertheless, he answered the call. He completed the tour in Dover but the strain had been too much. He died towards midnight on 3 April 1253.

His body was brought back to Chichester and buried, as he had wished, before the altar of St Edmund in the north aisle of the nave. People flocked to pray at his tomb. 'The people's Saint' was formally canonised in 1262 and five years later, on 16 June, in the presence of King Edward I his body was processed ('translated') to a new shrine behind the High Altar. For nearly 300 years, until its destruction in 1538 during the Reformation, his shrine was an important centre of pilgrimage.

It wasn't until 1930 that the restoration of the shrine commenced, but since then a new altar has been installed (1984), the Anglo-German Tapestry hung behind it (1985) and a relic of St Richard, returned from an abbey in Normandy, interred beneath it (1992). 'St Richard's Prayer', known by generations of Sussex people, is a living testament to his life:

> Thanks be to thee,
> my Lord Jesus Christ,
> for all the benefits which
> thou hast given me,
> for all the pains and insults
> which though has borne for me.
> O most merciful Redeemer,
> Friend and Brother,
> may I know thee more clearly,
> love thee more dearly,
> and follow thee more nearly.
> Amen.

('Prayer of St Richard', Bishop of Chichester, 1245–53.)

Fast forward some seven centuries and we come to a forward-looking dean who significantly added to the 'Work of human hands ...' which are such a notable feature within the cathedral. The dean has wide-ranging responsibilities. These include responsibility for the cathedral buildings and their contents. To quote from the Church of England job specification, 'the presentation and interpretation of its heritage ... to have oversight of the cathedral's development ... the care of the fabric'.

Dean Walter Hussey (Dean of Chichester, 1955–77) significantly revived the role of the Church as a patron of the arts. He commissioned new works for the cathedral. This was a continuation of the artistic patronage that Hussey had begun as vicar in his Northamptonshire church. In Northampton he had commissioned an anthem from Benjamin Britten, a 'Madonna and Child' by Henry Moore, and a 'Crucifixion' by Graham Sutherland. Since the dean is also responsible for the cathedral's finances at Chichester this gave him the wherewithal to continue his mission. He believed in the power of art to deliver the Christian message, very much as did his predecessors pre-Reformation.

In Chichester, he was able to build upon an impressive, existing body of work. This ancient 'Work of human hands ...' (a phrase taken from a prayer used in the Holy Communion service), is the subject of Verse 4. The twelfth-century 'Lazarus Reliefs' include a depiction of Martha, sister of Lazarus, who witnessed his raising from the dead. They are regarded as outstanding examples of pre-Gothic sculpture, unique in English architecture. Martha's faith in Christ and his divine power on this occasion is said to be the origin for Jesus' famous words, 'I am the resurrection and the life' (John 11: 25).

Other ancient treasures include a fragment of a Roman mosaic pavement, viewable through a glass window, and fourteenth-century medieval misericords on the undersides of hinged seats in the choir stalls. When the seat was turned up, the skilfully carved misericords provided a ledge upon which to perch. Medieval services involved long periods standing. The literal meaning of the term 'misericord' is 'act of mercy'. At odds with their surroundings, the carvings often depicted secular or even pagan images or scenes. The set of thirty-eight in Chichester Cathedral survived the destruction of the Reformation.

In the transepts, which are the crosspieces of a cruciform (cross-shaped) church, are Tudor paintings by Lambert Barnard (1485–1567), a local painter. These are on two huge wooden panels (14ft x 32ft). They were recently restored (HRH Prince of Wales was a patron of the appeal) and are of national importance: 'A sophisticated piece of political theatre and propaganda, giving us a rare opportunity to imagine how Henry VIII was seen by his ordinary subjects, in contrast to the courtly art of the period' (official Chichester Cathedral website). The 'political' importance to the cathedral was that it showed King Henry VIII conferring royal protection on Chichester Cathedral – both flattery and an insurance policy. To further establish the cathedral's status the paintings include an imposing array of portraits of past bishops and the kings and queens of England.

The lines 'The earl and countess lie in stone' and 'What will survive of us is love' are taken from Philip Larkin's poem 'An Arundel Tomb', published in 1964 in his collection *The Whitsun Weddings*. This fourteenth-century table tomb in Chichester Cathedral depicts the Earl and Countess of Arundel lying side by side and, uniquely, holding hands. Larkin found this 'extremely affecting' but he also scribbled, at the bottom of one draft, 'Love isn't stronger than death just because statues hold hands for 600 years'. Larkin had a reputation for gloomy cynicism!

The modern 'Work of human hands' (Verse 5) relates to Dean Walter Hussey's acquisitions. These include paintings by Graham Sutherland and Patrick Procktor, sculpture by Philip Jackson and John Skelton, tapestries by John Piper and Ursula Benker-Schirmir and a stained-glass window by Marc Chagall. The latter is based on the theme of Psalm 150, '... let everything that hath breath praise the Lord' – used in the penultimate line of the poem.

There are other notable works of art in the cathedral, both 'Ancient & Modern'. (This phrase also alludes to the hymnbook, 'Hymns Ancient and Modern'):

> All modern art is controversial: each of Walter Hussey's commissions aroused great passions at the time, but they have, without exception, become greatly loved ... the unique spirit of this Cathedral ... contemporary art in an ancient setting, for which Chichester has become known all over the world. (The Very Reverend Nicholas Frayling, Dean of Chichester Cathedral.)

Hussey also amassed an extraordinary private collection from his own means. This was the basis for the founding of Pallant House Gallery in Chichester, one of the must-see galleries on the south coast.

Finally ... 'and Music'. Organ music has been a feature since medieval times. There are now five organs of different sizes and styles in the cathedral. The pipes of the main organ date back to the Restoration, over three centuries ago. The most modern is a digital electronic organ. One notorious incumbent of the post of cathedral organist, from 1602 until his death in 1623, was the brilliant composer of madrigals, Thomas Weelkes. His compositions were spirited, imaginative and very popular. It would have been a breath of fresh air. A parallel today might be with some of the joyful new hymns such as 'Shine Jesus Shine' (Graham Kendrick, 1987). Weelkes composed more Anglican services than any of his contemporaries and his back catalogue is still a present-day resource.

However, Weelkes was the 'bad boy' musician of his time. As Ian Mortimer puts it in *The Time Traveller's Guide to Elizabethan England*, 'Weelkes is the nearest thing to an Elizabethan rock 'n' roller, famous for his drunkenness, blasphemy and bad behaviour ... On one occasion during evensong he urinates from the organ loft on the dean below'.

In more recent times, although the organists have been less notorious, Chichester has still been ground-breaking. Anne Maddocks (assistant organist, 1942–49) was the first woman in the country to hold such a post in a cathedral.

The Prebendal School Choir currently sings for eight services each week, continuing a tradition started by Bishop Sherburne in the fifteenth century. This is further supported by guest choirs from parishes and elsewhere. The popular lunchtime concerts (some people take sandwiches) are listed in the events programme.

The 'Chichester Psalms' were another result of Dean Hussey's commissioning. In December 1963 he wrote to Leonard Bernstein requesting a piece for the cathedral's August 1965 music festival. When in Northampton, he had already successfully commissioned Benjamin Britten to write the cantata 'Rejoice in the Lamb'. To Leonard Bernstein, he wrote:

> I do realise how enormously busy you are, but if you could manage to do this we should be tremendously honoured and grateful ... Many of us would be very delighted if there was a hint of *West Side Story* about the music. (Letter from Dean Walter Hussey to Leonard Bernstein, December 1963.)

Although on a sabbatical from his post as Music Director of the New York Philharmonic, Bernstein was indeed very busy:

> I spent almost the whole year writing 12-tone music and even more experimental stuff. I was happy that all these new sounds were coming out: but after about six months of work I threw it all away. It just wasn't my music; it wasn't honest. The end result was the Chichester Psalms which is the most accessible, B-flat majorish tonal piece I've ever written. (Bernstein's comments during a 1977 press conference.)

He even expressed these feelings in a poem submitted to the *New York Times* on 24 October 1965:

> For hours on end I brooded and mused
> On materiae musicae, used and abused;
> On aspects of unconventionality,
> Over the death in our time of tonality ...
> Pieces for nattering, clucking sopranos
> With squadrons of vibraphones, fleets of pianos
> Played with the forearms, the fists and the palms –
> And then I came up with the Chichester Psalms.
> ... My youngest child, old-fashioned and sweet.
> And he stands on his own two tonal feet.

The piece blends biblical Hebrew verse with the Christian choral tradition. It is a musical depiction of the composer's hope for brotherhood and peace. It is in turns jazzy, melodic, gentle, violent, tuneful and dissonant. As Dean Hussey had requested, there was even music cut from *West Side Story*. Dean Hussey had his music for the Chichester Cathedral Music Festival.

Finally, 'The popstars in the nave –'. What is that about? The cathedral has hosted not only classical performances. Such diverse musicians as Pink Floyd, Bob Geldof and the Hollies have enlivened the nave. 'But would Gustav turn in his grave?' A memorial to the English composer Gustav Holst (1874–1934), known particularly for 'The Planets Suite', is set into the floor of the north transept, where lie his ashes. Holst often visited the cathedral for music festivals. Just a few feet from Holst's memorial is that to 'bad boy' Thomas Weelkes, whose music, if not his behaviour, Holst admired. Perhaps not such unlikely bedfellows after all!

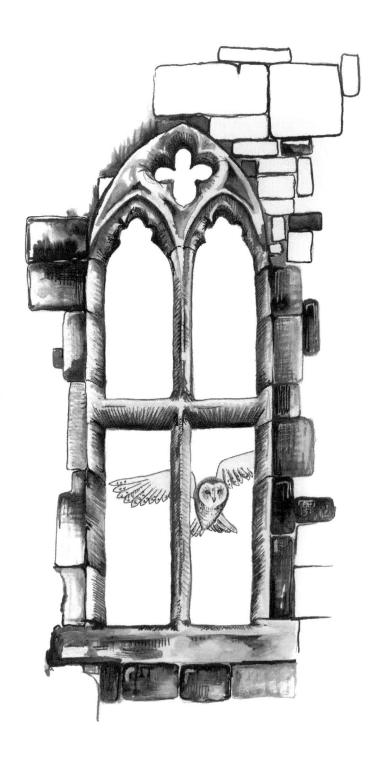

THE CHRISTMAS CASTLE

From Sussex Downs to Sussex coast, conquered lands.
The fortress on the hilltop, the watchful eye,
reward from a king, returned to a king.
Changing hands, changing tastes,
restructured, remodelled, renewed,
fit for a dancing queen.

Ancestry, eight fifty years of dukes and earls,
Norfolk in Sussex.
Defenders of the Crown,
Defenders of the Faith.
The worst of times, heads rolled,
the poet earl, the Plotting Duke,
Mary, Anne and Katherine, ill-fated queens.

Shadows, ghosts,
the founder earl, the watching eye,
the broken-hearted lover,
atop the tower,
the Blue Man browsing books,
the servant scrubbing pots,
the small white bird ...
foretelling death.

A collector's garden, a collector's pride,
A consort casting envious eyes.
But lost to time. Until
the car park supplanted, the garden replanted,
once more evergreen,
once more players in
Oberon's Palace.

Battles, jousts, crossed swords, crossed lances,
leather on willow,
and the castle the stand-in star.

13

ARUNDEL CASTLE
FAMILY HOME OF THE DUKES OF NORFOLK

Why 'The Christmas Castle'? The founder of the first castle at Arundel, Earl Rodger de Montgomery, was awarded his Sussex 'conquered lands' by William the Conqueror on Christmas Day 1067 – quite a Christmas present! The extensive holdings included the site of the present castle, which over the centuries has grown to become the second largest castle in England. Rodger was a cousin of the new king and they had been best friends since childhood. Rodger had stayed behind in Normandy to look after William's holdings there while his cousin went off to invade England.

Arundel was one of the first of a series of fortresses that the Normans built to secure their new lands. Rodger's specific task was to guard the southern coast and the River Arun against invaders. Rodger's son and successor, though, Robert de Belleme, was not a king's man. He unsuccessfully sided against King Henry I, was banished and the castle 'returned to a king'. This seemed to set a pattern, the castle occasionally 'changing hands' between the Crown and the Earls of Arundel over a period of some 400 years.

The Fitzalan family (Earls of Arundel) gained the castle by marriage in 1243. It then passed, again by marriage, to the Howards (the Dukes of Norfolk) in 1555, who have held onto it ever since. The proud owners of the castle are remembered by a series of portraits by leading artists of the day – Van Dyck, Mytens, Gainsborough, Reynolds and Lawrence.

Both families, however, had some significant fallings out with the monarchs of the day. On the positive side, 'Defenders of the Crown', Richard, the first Fitzalan Earl of Arundel, became good friends with King Edward I, 'Longshanks'. He had fought with him against the Scots (1300). The king described him as 'A handsome and well-loved Knight, I saw there richly armed in red with gold lion rampant' (*Rolls of the Siege of Caerlaverock*). And so it continued. Successive earls and dukes fought on the side of the Crown against the French (Battle of Crecy and the Hundred Years War), the Welsh (pursuing Owain Glyn Dŵr), the Scots again (Flodden), the Spanish (the Armada, with Sir Francis Drake), in the War of the Roses, the English Civil War and the Boer War.

On the negative side, the 2nd and 4th Earls and 4th Duke ('the Plotting Duke') were beheaded for treason, as was Henry Howard (1516–47), the Tudor courtier and 'poet earl'. The 13th Earl died in the Tower of London for his faith. He was canonised in 1970.

The female relations didn't fare too well either, 'Mary [Queen of Scots], Anne [Boleyn] and Katherine [Howard], ill-fated queens'. All were also beheaded. The rosary that Mary carried to her execution is on display in Arundel Castle.

The 'poet earl', cousin of Ann Boleyn, also left a legacy. With Thomas Wyatt he is credited with bringing the Italian sonnet form to England and he was also one of the first to write in unrhymed blank verse. Both forms were subsequently raised to new heights by William Shakespeare, leader of the next generation of poets and playwrights.

'Changing tastes / restructured, remodelled, renewed' refers to the many transformations that the castle has undergone since the first motte and double bailey design was completed in 1068. The plan is very similar to that of the later Windsor Castle, which explains why Arundel is often used by filmmakers as a stand-in for Windsor – 'the castle the stand-in star' (last line). The castle has been used in the 2009 film *The Young Victoria*, *The Madness of King George* and even in a *Dr Who* episode, 'The Silver Nemesis' (1988) in which the Cybermen, as opposed to Civil War soldiers, are the enemy.

The first makeover was to replace the original timbers with stone. The barbican was built at the end of the thirteenth century, as was the square well tower in the keep. The former certainly strengthened the defences, surviving a battering in the English Civil War. The walls are pockmarked with the impressions of cannon balls. Another 100 years passed before the addition of the Fitzalan Chapel, in Early English Gothic style, in accordance with the will of the 3rd Earl of Arundel, hero of the Battle of Crecy. Another fine example of the Gothic style is the library.

In 1787, Charles Howard (1746–1815), the 11th Duke of Norfolk began a necessary restoration. He was known as the 'Drunken Duke', perhaps an occupational hazard as a friend of the Prince Regent. He bought hundreds of acres of land north of the estate, enclosing it with high walls, lodges and drives. His deer park was one of the favourite subjects for the artists J.M.W. Turner and John Constable. It was at this time also that the folly, Hiome's Tower, was built. The duke also extended the castle, adding bedrooms and dressing rooms to the courtyard side of the gallery. These were later refurbished by the 13th Duke (1791–1856) for the visit of Queen Victoria in 1846 and so are known as the Victoria and Albert Rooms.

There was, in fact, a major remodelling of the castle during the Victorian period, first in the English nineteenth-century Gothic revival style and subsequently in a more straightforward style – 'changing tastes'. Arundel was one of the first English country houses to provide the modern comforts of electricity, central heating, service elevators and integral firefighting equipment. Henry, the 15th Duke (1847–1917) was the driving force. He would have been completely in sympathy with the current emphasis on Health & Safety. The castle is now fully restored and is still the family home of the Howards, Earls of Arundel and Dukes of Norfolk. The castle is a grade one listed building and a member of the Historic Houses Association.

The Duke of Norfolk is England's Premier Duke and the Earl Marshall of England, responsible for the organisation of state ceremonial occasions. 'Defenders of the Faith' additionally refers to the historical role of the families of the Dukes of Norfolk as this country's leading Roman Catholics. Among the 10,000 books in the library is an extensive collection on Catholic history. The Fitzalan Chapel, founded in 1380, was separated from the parish church in 1879 by a glass wall in order that it could continue as an independent Catholic ecclesiastical structure. The chapel contains the tombs of Earls of Arundel and Dukes of Norfolk. A number of masses are said at the chapel each year for the dukes' souls, as intended by the founder, the 3rd Earl of Arundel.

Over the centuries in which Arundel Castle was occupied by the Earls of Arundel and Dukes of Norfolk, depending upon the religious convictions of the monarch of the time, it was either 'the best of times' or 'the worst of times'. The phrase is taken from the opening paragraph of *A Tale of Two Cities* by Charles Dickens:

> It was the best of times, it was the worst of times, it was the age of wisdom, it was the age of foolishness, it was the epoch of belief, it was the epoch of incredulity, it was the season of Light, it was the season of Darkness, it was the spring of hope, it was the winter of despair.

Dickens' story opens in the year 1775, but similar see-sawing fortunes had been a familiar tale for the ancestors of the Earls of Arundel and Dukes of Norfolk for generations before.

Any self-respecting castle must have ghosts, and Verse 3 lists the 'shadows, ghosts' said to populate Arundel Castle. On the 'Castles of the World' website, in an article on Arundel, the researcher Carolyn D. Ahms recounts the stories. The founder Earl, Rodger de Montgomery, is said to haunt the keep, still keeping watch. Local legend recounts that a 'broken-hearted lover' jumped to her death from the top of one of the towers following the break-up of a love affair. The 'Blue Man' is a bit of a bookaholic, browsing since 1630 among the 10,000 tomes in the library. The 'servant scrubbing pots' was reputedly a kitchen lad who was treated very badly – in fact, eventually beaten to death. His ghost has continued scrubbing pots and pans for over two centuries. The 'small white bird' of tradition is perhaps not so small. Before the keep was restored a colony of white owls lived there. It is said that when a family member is about to die, one of these reappears outside one of the windows.

Verse 4 is in tribute to Thomas Howard, the 'Collector [14th] Earl' (1585–1646). He was responsible for many of the treasures in the castle, furniture and paintings (particularly portraits), and for the 'Collector Earl's Garden' in the grounds.

The 'consort casting envious eyes' was Prince Albert, husband of Queen Victoria. During their three-day visit in December 1846, not the best month to view a garden, the queen wrote in her journal, 'The garden is very pretty and full of evergreens, which made Albert extremely jealous for Osborne House'.

'Lost to time' reflects the social and economic changes following the Second World War, during which time the castle had been a base for British, Canadian and American troops. By the 1970s the garden was derelict and became a tarmac and concrete car-parking area. Now, however, 'the garden [is] replanted', but as an evocation of a Jacobean garden rather than a direct recreation of the original. It is a memorial to the 14th Earl.

The new Collector Earl's Garden was opened on 14 May 2008 by the Prince of Wales. There are many interesting features in the garden, one of which is Oberon's Palace. This is a green oak, seashell-lined version of a spectacle designed by Inigo Jones for Prince Henry's Masque on New Year's Day 1611. Open-air Shakespeare plays, no doubt including *A Midsummer Night's Dream*, are performed, perhaps to reconcile the King of the Fairies with his new abode.

'Battles, jousts, crossed swords, crossed lances' all refer to events in the castle's annual calendar. These provide professional historical interpretations of periods throughout the castle's history. The highlight is the jousting and medieval tournament week in the summer.

'Leather on willow' of course refers to the game of cricket, hopefully a less lethal form of combat. There has been a cricket field in the castle grounds since 1895. The Arundel Castle Cricket Club's picturesque ground is one of three used by Sussex County Cricket Club for county championship matches. It also hosts the Sussex Martlets CC, the Duke of Norfolk's XI and various celebrity and charity fixtures.

There remains perhaps one puzzling clue to solve, at the end of the first verse. The castle 'renewed/ fit for a dancing queen'. No, this is not the 'Dancing queen … only seventeen' of the well-known ABBA song. It is Queen Victoria, at the age of 27 and already with five of her nine children, but still young enough to be 'in the mood for dancing'. The occasion was the December 1846 visit of Queen Victoria and Prince Albert to Arundel Castle. It was not exactly a low-key private visit. 'The Royal couple were welcomed by the Mayor … a 21-gun salute from a battery in the home park and an illuminated sign across the wall of the keep reading "Welcome Victoria and Albert"' ('Castles of the World', website article on Arundel).

The apartments set aside for the royal visitors had been especially remodelled and refurnished and the 13th Duke had also specially commissioned a portrait of Queen Victoria in readiness for the visit (the duke and duchess had had two years' notice). On the last evening of their visit an entertainment was organised with music and dancing, 'concluding with a very merry country dance which I danced with the Duke' (Queen Victoria's journal). The experience that both queens would have had in common was 'the beat from the tambourine' ('Dancing Queen', ABBA) – in the 1840s English country-dance bands almost always included a tambourine player.

THE STAGE

'Fairytale Gothic mansion', 'fake medieval manor', 'glorious pastiche' –
From garden lover's home to stage designer's set.

Act One,
Performers from far-flung climes,
cast by the banker and the plantsman,
partners, promoters, love's labour's found.

Act Two,
Scene I. The House – the Fire.
A library lost, flowers on paper, flowers in flames.
Scene II. The Garden – written through time,
alive in summer borders, in scents of roses, remembered names.

Act Three.
Midsummer Night's Dreams,
Pimms and picnics, games on the lawns,
winter nights, winter's tales,
draw closed the curtains,
draw back the curtains on a smaller stage.

Act Four.
The tempest,
more than the wind in the willows.
Four hours to fell four hundred years,
Redwoods, greenwoods, stand or fall –
a puzzle cracked, puzzle no more.

The Epilogue.
The challenge met, the woodland healed –
butterflies, dragonflies,
birds singing, children laughing.

The bookshop by the flower bed,
the workshop in the potting shed,
the croquet on the lawn,
revised, reborn.

We are now the players.
The stage awaits,
no curtain falls.

14

NYMAN'S

ONE OF THE FINEST NATIONAL TRUST GARDENS

Four generations of the Messel family have developed Nyman's. The four 'Acts' of the poem connect with scenes from their lives. The format also reflects the family's tradition of open-air summer theatre in the garden, a tradition still continued by the National Trust. Originally primarily Shakespeare plays, by 2013 the range extended from Shakespeare and Jane Austen, via trips to *Treasure Island* and Toad Hall, to a case for Sherlock Holmes.

The romantic ruins of the house provide a readymade backdrop to the action. The poem's opening line quotes from various writers' first impressions of Nyman's. Simon Jenkins, in *England's Thousand Best Houses*, speaks of the 'spectacular gardens', acknowledged as some of the finest in National Trust stewardship and still reflecting the vision of the garden-loving first generation. Among the highlights are the rose garden in June, the 'iconic' double summer borders, the walled garden – the oldest part – and the wisteria pergola next to the croquet lawn. It is a garden for all seasons and as such is kept open by the National Trust all year (apart from Christmas Day and Boxing Day).

The house itself, however, is now a shadow of its past, mainly due to a disastrous fire. Continuing the garden theme, though, a ruined section of the house has been taken over by what is claimed to be one of the biggest rambling roses anywhere on house walls. This prompted Jenkins to refer to Nyman's as 'England's Ankor' (Angkor Wat, originally overgrown by vegetation, is a Hindu temple complex in Cambodia, a must-see sight for tourists). As outdoors, so also indoors. In June the remaining habitable rooms of the house are taken over by an exhibition of the florist's art.

Ludwig and Anne Messel bought the estate in the late nineteenth century 'to make a dream country home'. Ludwig, a banker, had moved to England from Germany. Having adapted the original Victorian mansion, he teamed up with his head gardener, James Comber, to create a 30-acre garden filled with plants brought back by the global plant hunters of the time.

In 1872 Jules Verne had published *Around the World in 80 days*, and inspired by this, together with the increasing opportunities for global travel, landowners competed to outdo their horticultural neighbours. In Ludwig's case these were the Loders (Leonardslee) and William Robinson (Gravetye). The fruits of the plant hunters' expeditions to 'far-flung climes' such as South America, the Far East, Burma and Tasmania, were 'love's labour's found' (not 'lost') in this case.

Ludwig died in 1915 and the estate passed to his son, Leonard. The care of the garden had been continued by Ludwig's daughter, Muriel, but tragically she died in 1918, aged 29. Leonard Messel and his wife Maud picked up the baton. In 1923, Leonard had the existing house pulled down and in its place built a large medieval-style manor, described as 'a glorious pastiche' in *Country Life* magazine. They had three children, Linley, Anne – who married Michael, 6th Earl of Rosse – and Oliver, who was to make his mark as an artist and stage designer.

Anne had inherited the gardening gene, these were golden years, but disaster was to strike the house. In 1947, on the morning of Leonard's 75th birthday, the household awoke to find Nyman's on fire. Leonard left and never revisited the house. Their collection of antique botanical books containing beautiful and irreplaceable illustrations was lost. The only record now is the living garden 'written through time'. 'Remembered names' refer to the lasting legacy of named species including Magnolia 'Leonard Messel', Camellia 'Leonard Messel' and Eucryphia 'Nymansay'. Colour illustrations of all three can be found in *The RHS New Encyclopaedia of Plants and Flowers*.

Act Three sees the next generation, Anne and Oliver, play their parts. Anne was the initiator of Shakespeare in the garden. The players were the local WI Dramatic Society. The poem alludes to *Love's Labour's Lost*, *A Midsummer Night's Dream*, *The Winter's Tale* and *The Tempest*, to connect with episodes in the life of the house and gardens:

I know a bank whereon the wild thyme blows,
Where oxlips and the nodding violet grows
Quite over-canopied with luscious woodbine,
With sweet musk-roses, and with eglantine:

(*A Midsummer Night's Dream*, William Shakespeare, extract from Oberon, King of the Fairies' speech, Act II, Scene I.)

As well as the summer theatre productions the National Trust also relives the days of 'Pimms and picnics, games on the lawns' in the summer events programme. Winter nights are remembered with a reference to one of stage designer Oliver's somewhat smaller stage sets. He furnished their TV screen with curtains, turning it into a miniature theatre proscenium! This is on view in one of the remaining rooms open to the public. When Oliver died on 13 July 1978 his ashes were placed under a memorial urn in the walled garden.

Oliver's nephew, Anthony Armstrong-Jones, is still also involved in the visual arts, as a world-renowned photographer. Among other achievements, he is famous for his portraits of notable people, including Queen Elizabeth II and the Duke of Edinburgh. There are over 100 of his photographic portraits in the National Portrait Gallery. It was as a result of his royal assignments that Armstrong-Jones got to know the queen's younger sister, the late Princess Margaret. They married on 6 May 1960 in Westminster Abbey. It was the first royal wedding to be broadcast on television. The following year Armstrong-Jones was granted the hereditary title of 1st Earl of Snowdon. The marriage was not to last and they divorced in 1978.

More recently, Lord Snowdon would have been a casualty of the 'clear-out' of hereditary peers from the House of Lords, but in 1999 in order to retain his seat he was created 'Baron Armstrong-Jones of Nyman's in the County of West Sussex', thus recognising his family's Sussex estate. As a life peer this enabled him to keep his seat in the Upper House.

In 1954, following Leonard's death, Nyman's had been handed over to the National Trust. However, this wasn't to be the end of the Messel family's connection. Enter the fourth, and present, generation. In 1987, Anne, Countess of Rosse and the mother of Lord Snowdon by her first husband, continued her involvement with the house as a director. Under the aegis of the National Trust she then handed over the family representation to another family member, Alistair Buchanan.

Just three days later came 'the Tempest' – the Great Storm of that year. Four hundred and eighty-six mature trees came down, some of which had been standing for over 400 years. Among the casualties was a giant Monkey Puzzle tree. This tree was believed to be the inspiration for the one featured in E.H. Shepard's illustration of the garden of Toad Hall in *The Wind in the Willows*. Ernest Shepard was a family friend of the Messels in the 1920s and early 1930s and had made sketches in the house and gardens.

Finally, 'The Epilogue' celebrates Nyman's present and looks to the future. Alistair Buchanan and his team successfully restored the woods and gardens after the storm. The woods are now a Site of Special Scientific Interest (SSSI), home to breeding birds, butterflies, dragonflies, woodland flowers and rare plants. The gardens again ring with the laughter of children playing in dens and tepees as in the days of the Messel children. For added fun there is a bamboo jungle. Nyman's is also now home to a secondhand bookshop, arts & crafts workshops and exhibitions in the potting shed, an excellent cafe and equipment for croquet and badminton for visitors' use on the lawns – 'We are now the players …'.

VENI. VIDI. VICI

Two sites, one heritage
linked by a path to a summer sun.

Scholars, digging through time,
stains underground
revealing a residence fit for a king.
Stane overground,
unwavering route to a rich man's home.

Uncovered, underfoot,
Cupid on a Dolphin,
Medusa,
Venus and the Gladiators,
Ganymede
being carried by an eagle.

Polychrome replacing monochrome,
new fashions –
but still set in stone.

Discovered, replanted,
Box hedges,
violets and roses,
fruit trees,
the cherry and the grape.

Plunderers or benefactors?
Invasion, occupation, retreat.
To conquer and to civilise.
But a loveless marriage?

For better,
– Houses, gardens, roads, cities, laws, trade,
the education of a people.
For worse,
– Lost freedoms,
a people dependant, defenceless,
no longer skilled in war.
Dark Ages.

15

FISHBOURNE ROMAN PALACE AND GARDENS & BIGNOR ROMAN VILLA

The poem title, a Latin phrase originally coined by Julius Caesar, translates as 'I came, I saw, I conquered'. It is from a message he sent back to the Senate in Rome following an overwhelming and swift (four hours) victory at the end of May, 47 BC. This put a stop to an insurgency in what is now modern north-eastern Turkey. The phrase is often also used in connection with Caesar's invasion of Britain in 55 BC, although it wasn't until the further invasion under the Emperor Claudius in AD 43 that the full-scale Roman occupation of Britain really got under way. This took a great deal longer.

The two sites, Fishbourne and Bignor, both Roman dwellings constructed during the Roman occupation (AD 43–410), lie within reach of the Roman road known as Stane Street. This ran from Noviomagnvs (Chichester) to London. The present-day roads on sections of the route are the A285 and A29. As Graham Robb points out in *The Ancient Paths*, although major Roman roads are usually noted for being ruler straight – the motorways of their day – Stane Street sets off from Eastgate in Chichester in the wrong direction, towards the village of Pulborough. Only there does it correct itself and aim towards its intended destination, London Bridge, 'The inescapable conclusion is that the road from Noviomagnvs [Chichester] was originally aimed, not at Londinium, but at the Celtic port of Durobrivae [Rochester] on the river Medway'.

Robb goes on to explain that the two Celtic tribes around Chichester and Rochester had strong trading ties with Gaul (France) before the arrival of the Romans. The routes of Celtic roads owed much to earlier Druidic wisdom. The original 22km from Chichester to Pulborough is oriented on the summer solstice. The Romans just possibly made use of a convenient stretch of this existing Celtic road – 'a path to a summer sun'.

It was in 1960 that the archaeologist Barry Cunliffe first systematically excavated Fishbourne Roman Palace. The site is now in the care of the Sussex Archaeology Society. As with most Roman villas, the palace evolved over several centuries, starting from around AD 75, on the site of what was originally a timber-built Roman Army supply base, and continuing until it was burnt down around AD 270. Following the fire, much of the masonry was cannibalised for use in other buildings – perhaps some even found its way to the site of Bignor Roman Villa, which developed from a simple timber farm structure to a stone building from the middle of the third century.

The first three centuries AD saw a Roman housebuilding boom, extending beyond Italy and including Britain and Gaul. In the heart of Rome itself, Sir Mortimer Wheeler in *Roman Art and Architecture*, describes how the Emperor Nero, between AD 64 and AD 68, had built a vast country palace which even included a lake on the site of the subsequent Colosseum. This didn't go down very well! 'All Rome is transformed into a villa!' (*Suetonius*, Nero, XXXIX.)

Although nowhere near the same scale, Fishbourne Roman Palace is the largest Roman residence so far discovered in Britain and possibly north of the Alps. H.H. Scullard, in *Roman Britain: Outpost of the Empire*, was among those to suggest that it was indeed 'fit for a king', namely Cogidubnus (*c*. AD 45–80), the pro-Roman heir of King Verica of the Atrebates, the dominant local Celtic tribe. Cogidubnus was installed as a client king by the Romans. Evidence of his Romanisation is to be found on an inscription on a temple he authorised at Chichester. This was funded by a local guild, but dedicated to two Roman deities:

> To Neptune and Minerva, for the welfare of the Divine House [i.e Roman Imperial House], by the authority of Tiberius Claudius Cogidubnus, Great King in Britain, the college of artificers and those therein erected this temple from their own resources [...]ens, son of Prudentinus, donated the site.
>
> (A translation from the Latin by J.E. Bogaers, *Britannia*, 1979.)

Fishbourne Roman Palace had a larger footprint than does Buckingham Palace today, whereas Bignor Roman Villa was the Romano-British equivalent of a Victorian country house and estate, with around 2,000 acres of arable land as well as extensive pasturage.

'Uncovered, underfoot' and on display at the two sites are the two best collections of in-situ undercover Roman mosaics in Britain. '*Cupid on a Dolphin*' (Fishbourne), '*Medusa*' (both sites), '*Venus and the Gladiators*' (Bignor) '*Ganymede being carried by an eagle*' (Bignor)' refer to the subjects of some of the best-known mosaics.

Mosaic floors were the must-have interior decorations of the day, together with wall paintings (as can be seen at Pompeii and Herculaneum). As with all decorating fashions throughout the ages, it was necessary for those who could afford it to keep up to date. The first, black and white, mainly geometrical, mosaics were replaced by coloured mosaics, often of Roman gods and myths, just as in the twentieth-century advances in technology enabled us to replace black and white television sets with colour. It is less common to find original monochrome mosaics, but fine polychrome examples abound at both sites, sometimes laid on top of earlier monochrome mosaics. Bignor Roman Villa also contains the longest mosaic on display in Britain, a Greek key pattern mosaic in the 79ft north corridor.

'Stains underground' also revealed evidence of Britain's first formal garden on the Fishbourne Palace site. Part of this has been replanted using the original bedding trenches. Although only pollen from weeds could be found, the present planting is based on descriptions of his own garden by the Roman writer, Pliny, and other plants known to be of Italian origin. The Roman Garden Museum even contains a reconstructed Roman garden shed complete with tools.

Bignor Roman Villa had been discovered in 1811 when a farmer's plough hit a large stone. The site was excavated by John Hawkins, who lived nearby at Bignor Park, together with a leading antiquary, Samuel Lysons. It opened as a popular tourist attraction to the public in 1814. This was some 150 years before the excavation of Fishbourne Roman Palace and gardens.

'Plunderers or benefactors?' marks the essence of a change in attitudes to the Roman occupation. This change took place during the nineteenth and early twentieth centuries, as reflected in the schoolbooks of the time. In 1841 in *Daily Lesson Book No IV*, 'The cheapest and most comprehensive Class Book yet offered to the public', children were taught:

> The Roman Generals went abroad to subdue other countries for no other purpose than to acquire fame and spoils for themselves, and power for Rome. They slaughtered the inhabitants without mercy, they robbed them without scruple, and they subjected them to the Roman yoke without the slightest regard to the rights of mankind.
>
> *(Daily Lesson Book No. IV, adopted in the schools of the British and Foreign School Society.)*

By 1874, in *Little Arthur's History of England*, although the view of the early years of the Roman occupation had been toned down somewhat, it was still essentially negative, '… the poor Britons were very unhappy, because they had lost their freedom, and could never do as they liked'. But regarding the later years of the occupation, children were taught that things had changed for the better:

> [God] put it into the hearts of the Romans to teach the Britons most of the things they knew themselves … to build houses and walls of stone or brick, to spin and weave wool, to make better clothes, to wash properly and keep their hair neat, to wear ornaments, to grow corn to make bread and to cultivate gardens. The Romans also built schools and developed cities, markets and trade.

As Francis Pryor points out in *Britain AD*, the 'Sub-emperor' of Britain and Gaul at the time, Constantius I, was not anti-Christian, nor was his son, Constantine the Great, who in AD 313 in his *Edict of Milan* guaranteed total religious toleration throughout the Roman Empire. Also, the stated mission of the occupying Roman general, Julius Agricola (from AD 78), had been not just to conquer but to civilise. (Agricola's operations and works are known to us through the descriptions by his son-in-law, Tacitus, the Roman historian.)

By 1904, children were being taught:

Britain was the better for having been ruled by Rome. [There was a downside though] The use of arms was forbidden to the conquered race, and the effect was that the Britons soon ceased to be the brave and warlike people they had been. When [the Romans] departed they left a poor, spiritless people, a nation unskilled in war and unfit to take care of themselves.

(*McDougall's Preparatory Historical Reader*, Waverley School Series.)

By AD 410 the Roman Empire was showing signs of breaking up and so the Emperor Honorius commanded a withdrawal of his legions from Britain to help in defending the centre. Many of the Roman soldiers who had put down roots in Britain were distraught:

Legate, I had the news last night – my cohort ordered home
By ship to Portus Itius and thence by road to Rome.
I've marched the companies aboard, the arms are stored below:
Now let another take my sword. Command me not to go!
[...]
Legate, I come to you in tears – my cohort ordered home!
I've served in Britain forty years. What should I do in Rome?
Here is my heart, my soul, my mind – the only life I know.
I cannot leave it all behind. Command me not to go!

(*The Roman Centurion's Song*, Rudyard Kipling, first and last verses.)

The Romans' withdrawal was the signal for a general attack upon 'the poor defenceless Britons' from all points of the compass.

It was the beginning of what came to be known as the Dark Ages.

MASTERPIECE

Time for change, a country house, a family house.
Midland money, forest vision,
Nonconformist, progressive,
cultured, concerned ...
for better lives.

Hollybush reincarnated. Medieval meets modern.
Rustic echoes, trademark styles.
Tile-hung, pebble-dashed, weather-boarded.
Dormers, chimneys, the Sixpenny Room.
In with the old and in with the new.

Flowers, fruits, stems and leaves
in rooms in the house,
in rooms in the garden.

Feeding the family, feeding the senses,
nature gently tamed.
Croquet on the lawn,
tea on the terrace.
Philip the planner, Margaret the planter,
shared visions. Masterpiece.
halcyon days.

And inside as out. Masterpiece.
All the arts, all the crafts, together,
art beyond the easel.
William ... designer, reformer, poet.
Philip ... creator, conservator, hero.
Taking from the past, gifting to the present,
the useful, the beautiful.

For us, the house, the time capsule,
For us, the garden revival,
the Firm renewed, and still, for us,
the Sussex Chair.

16

STANDEN HOUSE AND GARDEN
AN ARTS AND CRAFTS FAMILY HOME

Built in the 1890s, Standen was the home of the Beale family from 1894 to 1972, before passing to the National Trust. The house occupies an idyllic site overlooking Weirwood Reservoir, Ashdown Forest and the Sussex High Weald. It is one of the best surviving examples of an Arts and Crafts late Victorian home open to the public. It is a grade one listed building. Standen (his last) and the Red House in Bexleyheath (his first) are the only two remaining Webb houses open to the public and in the care of the National Trust.

Standen was built as a country home for James and Margaret Beale and their seven children. James was a solicitor, originally from Birmingham, who made his money by negotiating for the Midland Railway to build its main line through to St Pancras in London. The family were Nonconformist Christians and were socially progressive. They espoused many of the interests and concerns of their time. They were in touch with the movements working towards better lives for women and the lower classes. This latter is evident in the care that went into the design of the servants' areas at Standen.

They placed great importance on education. Their own desire for knowledge encompassed both the arts and the sciences. They undertook a world tour, mirroring the cultural grand tours of the eighteenth century. It was no wonder that they entrusted the creation of Standen to the like-minded partnership of Philip Webb and William Morris, leading figures in the Arts and Crafts Movement. Philip Webb also had a reputation for sticking to budget, which would have appealed to James Beale. This is not to say, though, that there was anything penny pinching about the project – only the best for Standen. The house took three years to build at a cost of £18,065 (about £2 million in today's money).

All the members of the family participated in the design discussions. Philip Webb was noted for making sure that his clients were fully consulted and felt involved. The Beale ladies embroidered the cushions in the house using Morris patterns. Margaret took a leading role in the garden design. The children also had their wishes granted.

James Beale was aged 50 when he embarked on the project. Standen was originally intended to be just a holiday and weekend retreat for the Holland Park-based Beale family, eventually becoming their retirement home. The house became the centre of their family life. James rode, hunted and played golf. Margaret, when not to be found in the garden, was entertaining their many friends and family members. The extensive gardens and their little playroom, the Sixpenny Room, provided their grandchildren with idyllic settings in which to give free rein to their imagination.

The Sixpenny Room is an illustration of how Philip Webb involved all family members in the design of the house. Helen Beale was aged just 8 and was the youngest daughter when she asked Webb to build her a 'little room' at the far end of the conservatory. He agreed – and charged her sixpence. The room became the headquarters of 'secret society' meetings for two generations of children. Their rocking horse, Dobbin, is also still to be found in the billiard room. With up to six excited children riding it at a time, though, this probably wasn't its original pasture.

Standen was a very happy house. Visitors often remark that one can sense this and still feel the warmth of the family's welcome today.

The second verse considers the style of the house. Hollybush Farmhouse was one of the original dwellings on the site. Webb incorporated the original tile-hung farmhouse, dating from about 1450, into his 1891 design, which became a set of architectural variations on the theme of that and other local dwellings – 'Rustic echoes'. The exterior uses an extraordinary mix of vernacular materials and styles – tile hanging, pebbledash, weatherboarding, stone and brick. To traditional architects of the day it would have seemed to be a jumble of the classical and the innovative, a bit of a mongrel. Elements of Queen Anne and Elizabethan were mixed in with Webb's signature dormers and tall chimneys. Despite the historic influences though, Standen was a thoroughly modern home with electricity and central heating. Somehow it all worked.

Moving now to the interior decoration of the house and to its garden, the 'back to nature' element of the Arts and Crafts Movement can be seen. 'Flowers, fruits, stems and leaves' decorate rooms in the house as well as the garden 'rooms'. William Morris considered the two inseparable – 'a house should be clothed by its garden'.

The Beales had first asked a London landscape architect, George Simpson, to come up with a garden layout, but he drew up a formal geometrical plan. Also, he was not one for subtle colour schemes. The layout followed the 'gardenesque', high-maintenance style which had been in vogue for some fifty years. This was not to the taste of either the Beales or the house's architect, Philip Webb. Both preferred a newer approach, a mixture of natural styles combining the best of old and new. Webb produced an alternative, and this was accepted.

Following Webb's outline plan, Margaret Beale then played the lead role in designing the detail. Webb's plan embodied the concept of dividing the 12-acre garden into a number of 'outdoor rooms'. Each had a distinct theme or purpose – the Kitchen Garden, the Rosery, the Quarry Garden, the Croquet Lawn, the Top Terrace, with its viewpoint – a fully illustrated map is available for visitors. Sissinghurst Castle Garden in Kent and Hidcote in Gloucestershire, both also in the care of the National Trust, are famous examples of this approach.

Margaret employed the same principles of design to the garden as Webb and Morris had to the house. There was nothing fussy or contrived; simplicity and a natural appearance were the essence. Margaret did, however, enjoy experimenting with colourful and unusual plants and planting patterns and so the garden was not entirely what Webb had envisioned. Also, it was in an almost continual state of flux, after all, this is one of the joys of the long-stay gardener. In Margaret's case the synthesis of art and science showed itself in her approach to these experiments. All was recorded in her garden and weather diaries, kept from 1890 to 1934. Although a self-taught 'amateur' gardener she possessed the approach of a professional horticulturalist.

After Margaret's death in 1936, two years after her last garden diary entries, garden development ceased. Her daughters seemed happy to leave their mother's work unchanged. But of course plants grow, and a dwarf shrubbery soon became a 30ft view-blocking barrier. When the National Trust took over Standen in 1973 it was necessary to cut back drastically and redesign the garden for low maintenance. This, together with the aftermath of the 1987 Great Storm, meant that much of Margaret's vision had been lost. Starting in October 2012, a major five-year (£500,000) restoration project has been under way to once more unify an Arts and Crafts garden with an Arts and Crafts house.

Time that we went inside…

The Arts and Crafts Movement began in Britain around 1880. It brought together a wide range of artistic endeavours: architecture, painting, sculpture, design, calligraphy, typography, bookbinding, engraving, literature, music and drama. It was a reaction to the all-pervading industrialisation which was downgrading people's skills and, they believed, quality of life generally. The movement promoted the idea of the home as a work of art, celebrating traditional craftsmanship and the beauty of simple designs, mainly drawn from nature. Furthermore, Morris promoted the concept of groups of such craft workers living and working within small communities, revitalising them.

As a family country home, Standen was an ideal setting for the movement's 'art beyond the easel'. In Sussex, a local group of artists and craftsmen located themselves and their studios in the village of Ditchling, now the site of the Ditchling Museum of Art and Craft.

The two leaders of the movement most closely involved in the Standen project were William Morris (1834–96), who mainly focussed on interior design, and Philip Webb (1831–1915), the architect. In 1859, following his marriage to Jane Burden, a favourite model for the Pre-Raphaelite artists, William Morris commissioned his friend Philip Webb to build them a new home. Morris wanted a modern home but 'very medieval in spirit'. This was the first fruit of their collaboration, the Red House in Upton, now within Bexleyheath in the London Borough of Bexley. Morris and his artist friends saw to the furnishing and interior decorations. They so enjoyed the project that they established 'The Firm' (Morris, Marshall, Faulkner & Co.)

There was a lot of cross-fertilisation of ideas. Webb's eye for design extended not only to his buildings but to the small details within them, such as the ornamentation of a sideboard, glassware and stained-glass windows, embroideries and metal fittings. The well-known 'Trellis' wallpaper, as at Standen, is not only a depiction of a garden feature of Webb's but an example of his skill as a painter. Webb drew the birds; Morris was responsible for the roses.

Standen House and garden was Philip Webb's final masterpiece, the Red House his first. In between, he not only designed his favourite country houses, but a school (All Saints' and St Richard's C of E Primary School, Old Heathfield, East Sussex), office buildings and a church.

Webb was also a conservation pioneer and co-founded the Society for the Protection of Ancient Buildings (SPAB) in 1877:

> Modest, practical and a pioneering conservationist, Philip Webb is my architectural hero. While Morris was the public voice of the emerging conservation movement, Webb was its engine. He influenced generations of architects and designers. (Matthew Slocombe, Director of SPAB.)

Philip Webb died at Worth, Sussex, on 17 April 1915.

'William … designer, reformer, poet' – William Morris was a man of many parts. Although three years younger than his friend Philip Webb, he died some years before him on 3 October 1896, at the age of 62. He had burnt himself out. When asked the cause of death, one of his doctors replied that he died from 'simply being William Morris, and having done more work than most ten men'. The biographer E.P. Thompson, in *William Morris: Romantic to Revolutionary*, wrote, 'he is one of those men whom history will never overtake'. He was the torchbearer who ran his race ahead of his time.

Born into a wealthy family he attended public school (Marlborough) and Oxford University (Exeter College). Never one for the easy life, though, he had a passion for social reform, becoming a fully fledged revolutionary Socialist in middle age. He also harked back to earlier times. He had a passion for all things medieval.

Although best known nowadays for his ground-breaking fabric and wallpaper designs, as displayed at Standen, this was only one of his crusades. In addition to his involvement in the Socialist movement, he was an early environmentalist, a novelist and one of the best known and most prolific Victorian poets. When Alfred, Lord Tennyson, the Poet Laureate, died in 1892, Morris was approached as a possible candidate. He turned down the suggestion. He disliked the obligation to produce royal commemorative verse, 'I am sorry poor old Tennyson thought himself bound to write an ode on our fat Vic's Jubilee: have you seen it?' (Letter to Jenny Morris, William Morris's elder daughter, 1887.)

In the matter of interior design, Morris regarded the typical mass-produced output of the Victorian era as cheap, tasteless rubbish. His mission was to return to the elegance and honesty of medieval art and crafts. The vehicle for this was to be 'The Firm'. Each of the seven partners held one £20 share and agreed to produce a few items at their own expense. Morris was a bit stumped for cash, though, at the time, and so his mother lent the group £100 for the start of trading. Morris also came up with what would nowadays be hailed as the perfect marketing hook, 'Have nothing in your houses that you do not know to be useful, or believe to be beautiful'.

After some fourteen years of trading, however, all was no longer peace and light between the partners. Following arguments over finances, in 1875 The Firm was dissolved. However, the business was to continue as 'Morris & Co.', under William's sole ownership. He wrote, 'I have got my partnership business settled at last, and am sole lord and master now.'

The original Red Lion Square shop, and later the reformed company's show-room at 449 Oxford Street (1877), was the Habitat of its day, a one-stop shop, stocking must-have objects at (almost) affordable prices. This included the 'Sussex Chair'. The design was based on an old chair that Morris & Co.'s business manager, George Warington Taylor, discovered in Hastings, where he lived. It was recommended in an influential 1881 interior decorating book as 'excellent, comfortable and artistic'. An example may still be found in the upstairs corridor at Standen.

It was also after the company's reformation that many of the products began to expand upon the vegetative theme – flowers and fruits set amidst swirling stems and leaves. These are also very much in evidence in Standen House. The company was also not averse to bringing in complementary products from craftsmen who shared their principles. The notable examples at Standen are the ceramics produced by William De Morgan – vases, bowls, plates and tiles. It is sometimes said that 'good design is that which can be enjoyed without any effort'. William Morris and his friends and partners certainly proved this as their continuing popularity shows.

Standen's story, however, does not end with the passing of James and Margaret Beale, William Morris, Philip Webb and the other founders of the Arts and Crafts Movement. In 1936 the estate passed first to the Beales' daughter, Margaret, and then after her death in 1947 to their youngest daughter, Helen – she of the Sixpenny Room. Helen bought the house from the family trust and shortly before her own death in 1972 bequeathed it to the National Trust.

As stated in their handbook, the National Trust has dressed the house as for a weekend stay in 1925, so that visitors can imagine themselves as guests of the family. The five-year Garden Revival project will be complete in 2017, and of course the trust has ensured that the gardens still provide opportunities for children's play.

And those last two lines of the poem? After some difficult years, Morris & Co. was bought out by Arthur Sanderson & Sons for £400 in 1940. Following a further change of ownership, today's thriving business still embodies William Morris's vision in their product range, but unfortunately this does not include the Sussex Chair. However, having been sturdily constructed, original pieces do still come up in auctions or antique shops and so with a bit of tracking down … 'still, for us, the Sussex Chair'.

SUSSEX
PEOPLE

CHALK PATHS

Footsteps tracing brushstrokes,
leading us along chalk paths.
No longer held back,
no longer just a scene on a gallery wall.

The bite of the wind in our nostrils,
the song of the larks in our ears
brought life,
dancing, whistling,
driving ghosts from that ageless scene.

Lighthouses, lifeboats, bathing machines, beds, beaches, greenhouses –
a world of light, of pleasure.
Tea at Furlongs.
But a scene set on the eve of a darkening storm.

From white chalk of the south to white ice of the north,
from pale light on pale land to midnight sun on ink-black sea,
steaming North, wakes cleaving new paths.
Ice giants usurp chalk giants.
White horses, once glimpsed from chattering trains,
now chase the silenced ships.

Artist at war.
Farm implements no more.

Searchlights, aircraft, barrage balloons, ships' screws, submarines –
a world apart, excitement,
new sounds, sensations.

The rescue mission,
the final scene set on the dawn of the breaking storm.

A fruitless search for a missing plane.
Return to base –
three counted out,
two counted back.
Contact lost.

We are now the observers.
We are walking his chalk paths, dancing, whistling,
driving ghosts from that ageless scene.

And after the storm,
the table still set for tea at Furlongs.

17

ERIC RAVILIOUS
ARTIST

Eric Ravilious (1903–42) was among a group of artists, also including Edward Bawden and John Nash, who gained prominence between the two world wars. He was killed on 2 September 1942, aged 39, while working as an official war artist in Iceland. The plane he was in was lost on an air-sea rescue mission.

In his short life he produced a wide-ranging body of work: wood engravings, murals, lithographs, designs for furniture, glass and ceramics (Wedgwood), and watercolours. In recent years the latter, his distinctive watercolours, particularly his pre-war landscapes of the South Downs, quiet lanes, farmhouse interiors, ports and farm implements and then his wartime paintings, have gained particular recognition.

The son of an Eastbourne antique shop owner, following his time at the local grammar school he won a scholarship to the Eastbourne School of Art (1919–22) followed by another scholarship to the Design School of the Royal College of Art (1922–25), where his tutor was Paul Nash and his contemporaries included Edward Bawden, a great friend, Edward Burra and Henry Moore. According to his fellow students, he 'had a temperament made of sunshine'. His temperament informed his work. He was always cheerful, and constantly whistling. He loved dancing, tennis and pub games. His style has been described as 'friendly art ... timeless, radiating light and pleasure'.

In 1930 Ravilious married Tirzah Garwood ('Tush'), who was a student at Eastbourne School of Art, where he had been teaching part time. They first set up home in Earl's Court, then a riverside flat in Hammersmith, before moving to the Essex countryside with their great friends, Edward Bawden and his wife. However, Ravilious was always drawn back to the South Downs, staying at Furlongs, Peggy Angus's cottage, a gathering place for many artists and the subject of a number of his paintings.

Ravilious once said to Angus, 'It was lovely to be in a place where you can spit on the floor' (quoted by Paul Laity in his article 'Ups and Downs'). *Tea at Furlongs* (August 1939) was painted on the eve of the outbreak of the Second World War.

Chalk Paths (1935) was one of a group of watercolours including *Downs in Winter* (1934), *Waterwheel* (1934) and *Beachy Head* (1939) which particularly captured the quiet beauty of the South Downs. 'The long white roads are a temptation. What quests they propose! They take us away to the thin air of the future or to the underworld of the past.'

And about Beachy Head and its lighthouse he wrote, '... an immense bar of light on the sea is splendid and must be done'. (The resulting watercolour was

Beachy Head, reproduced in James Russell, *Ravilious in Pictures: Sussex and the Downs*, p.30.) A later group, *The Vale of the White Horse* (1939), *The Westbury Horse* (1939) and *The Wilmington Giant* (1939), revealed his fascination with chalk figures carved into the hillsides.

In 1940 he was appointed an official war artist. In the next two years he captured a wide variety of wartime scenes, spending time first with the Royal Navy, on the surface, in submarines and with the Fleet Air Arm, and subsequently with the Royal Air Force.

Since boyhood, Ravilious had longed to travel to the Polar Regions, reading books of Arctic explorations, collecting maps and images. In May 1940 his dream was realised; he was to sail north with the destroyer HMS *Highlander* to Norway and across the Arctic Circle to support the Allied assault on Narvick. A delighted letter home to his wife, Tirzah, provided confirmation that his dream had come true, 'The seas in the Arctic Circle are the finest blue you can imagine, an intense cerulean and sometimes almost black ... It was so nice working on deck long past midnight in bright sunshine.'

After 7,500 miles and four weeks at sea he returned home, safe but unsettled. In late August 1942 he jumped at the opportunity of another trip north, this time flying to Iceland. While standing shaving in his house in August 1942, he announced to Tirzah, 'I will go to Iceland, it is the promised land'.

He had been there less than two days when, at dawn on 2 September 1942, he joined a search for a missing plane, a Hudson Mark III which had disappeared the previous day while engaging a U-boat. Ravilious was an observer in one of three Hudsons, setting off in a breaking storm to sweep the area. The search was fruitless. Two of the Hudsons returned safely, but radio contact was lost with that carrying Ravilious. It failed to return:

> Lives of great men all remind us
> We can make our lives sublime,
> And, departing, leave behind us
> Footprints on the sands of time;

> (An extract from 'A Psalm of Life ...' by Henry Wadsworth Longfellow.)

ENIGMA

From Sussex school to wartime hut,
an enigma to solve an enigma,
a gentle giant, eccentric 'Prof',
but a colossus that begat a new world.
His was no artificial intelligence, no mind in the machine.

'Action this day',
bombes to save lives not take away.
And now, honoured for seventy-year secrets,
the enigma remains.

We are his midnight comrades, inheritors –
the second generation
feeding humming monsters through air-chilled nights,
the third generation
student hackers turned code-crackers,
and the next company of heroes,
teenage minds locked in Mortal Kombat, bedroom warriors.

Torch bearers for the long-distance runner, but a marathon cut short
by the apple of forbidden love.

Another age, remorse, regret.
A Briton of distinction, statues, memorials,
but you deserved so much better.

18

ALAN TURING

CODE BREAKER AND
FATHER OF COMPUTER SCIENCE

An 'enigma' is defined as 'a riddle; a puzzling person or thing' (Oxford English Dictionary, from the Greek). In this case, both meanings apply. Alan Turing was a puzzling person to many of his colleagues. The details of his wartime work were another puzzle, kept secret for seventy years beyond the end of the Second World War. And of course his code-breaking of Second World War German messages enciphered by the aptly named German Enigma machine was akin to solving an almost insoluble riddle.

Alan Mathison Turing OBE, FRS was born in Maida Vale, London, in 1912 while his father was on leave from the Indian Civil Service. During Turing's childhood years his parents travelled between Hastings and India. He attended St Michael's, a day school in St Leonards-on-Sea from the ages of 6 to 13. His headmistress recognised his mathematical talent immediately. His education continued at Sherborne in Dorset, King's College, Cambridge, and Princeton, before returning to Cambridge. During the Second World War he worked at the Government Code and Cypher School (GCCS) at Bletchley Park, the forerunner of the present, relocated GCHQ. He was head of Hut 8, the section responsible for cracking German naval codes and particularly their Enigma machine. 'You needed exceptional talent, you needed genius at Bletchley and Turing's was that genius' (historian and wartime code breaker, Asa Briggs, UK Channel 4 TV broadcast, *Britain's Greatest Code Breaker*, 21 November 2011).

Like many geniuses, Turing was a bit of an eccentric, known to his colleagues as 'Prof'. Jack Good, a colleague, is quoted as having said that in June each year, to combat hay fever Turing cycled to work wearing a gas mask, getting off his faulty bicycle at carefully counted intervals to adjust the chain before it came off. He never had it mended.

Bombes (not a misspelling) were the electromechanical machines that Turing developed in 1940 to crack the Enigma codes. His team had considerable success and significantly reduced shipping losses, but despite this were frustrated by lack of funds. Eventually they wrote directly to Winston Churchill, who fired off an immediate memo, 'ACTION THIS DAY. Make sure they have all they want on extreme priority and report to me that this has been done'. There were no more resource problems. By the end of the war over 200 bombes were in use.

Additionally, in 1942, although Turing was not directly involved, some of his techniques fed into that of another team, Tommy Flowers' work in developing

Colossus. This was one of the world's first programmable digital electronic computers. This further accelerated Bletchley's code-cracking.

It is widely accepted that Turing's contribution shortened the war by two years. In 1945 he was awarded the OBE by King George VI 'for wartime services'. The nature of this work, however, was kept secret. His papers setting out the mathematical processes underlying his code-cracking methods continued to be of such value to GCHQ that they were not declassified until April 2012:

> Until Turing came along with his wonderful work, our ships were being sunk by the German submarines at a rate of knots ... it was only when, thanks to Turing we could read the German U-boat code ... that was when the war really turned, because quite frankly we could have lost the war through starvation.
>
> (Conservative peer Baroness Trumpington, who worked at Bletchley Park with others, typing up the decoded messages, speaking on Radio 4's *Today* programme at the time of the announcement of Turing's royal pardon.)

After the war he refined his ideas on a 'Universal Machine' and in February 1946 presented a paper with the first detailed design of a stored program computer. This launched the development of the first generation of computers around the world. That done, he then turned his attention to the possibility of artificial intelligence, devising what we now know as the 'Turing Test', a form of which is still used on the internet today. This controversially argues that if a competent expert conversing with a remote computer, for example in a foreign language or playing chess against it, cannot tell it from a human being then the computer is 'intelligent'.

The next generations of computers replaced valves with transistors and then integrated circuits (chips) which power our present-day laptops, smart phones and tablets. Vast air-conditioned computer rooms housing humming cabinets as tall as their human operators, running day and night, came and went.

Elementary computer programs, laboriously entered as strings of noughts and ones (binary), developed first into systems underpinning most functions of business, government and industry, and now into the apps on our mobile phones. Computer games and the internet brought Turing's now truly 'Universal Machines' into our homes. Second World War battles can now be enacted bloodlessly in games like Company of Heroes and fighting skills honed in games such as Mortal Kombat. Every year such simulations grow more sophisticated and more closely approach Turing's definition of 'artificial intelligence'. 'From a very young age, I knew about the legend of Alan Turing – among awkward, nerdy teenagers, he is a patron saint' (Graham Moore, writer of the Academy award-winning screenplay of *The Imitation Game*, Black Bear Pictures, 2014.) GCHQ now even uses an online code-breaking test as a recruiting tool to attract talented hackers to work for them.

Sadly, Turing did not live to see any of this. In 1952, he pleaded guilty to committing a then criminal act of homosexuality. Given a choice between imprisonment and chemical castration, he chose the latter. His security clearance was removed, he was no longer able to continue with government work here and was denied entry into the United States. Although it was said that Turing had suffered the side effects of his chemical castration 'with good humour', it was assumed when he died that he subsequently decided to end his life.

Turing's friend, the author Alan Garner, writing in an article in *The Guardian* in 2011, supported a suggestion by Turing's biographer, Andrew Hodges, that Turing's 'fascination with the fairy tale "Snow White and the Seven Dwarfs" ... and the ambiguity of the poisoned apple' lay behind his choice of suicide method. It is commonly accepted that he chose to inject his regular bedtime apple with cyanide, ironically the poison also used by old enemies, among them Adolf Hitler, Eva Braun, Rommel and Himmler. On 8 June 1954, his cleaner found him dead, two weeks before his 42nd birthday, a half-eaten apple beside his bed. Although the apple itself was not tested for cyanide, the post mortem revealed cyanide poisoning as the cause of death and so this became the suspect.

At the time, though, Turing's mother believed that his death may have been a terrible accident due to her son's careless handling of a cyanide-using apparatus with which he was experimenting. This 'alternative explanation' was also put forward by Professor Jack Copeland, who later questioned the coroner's verdict.

Over the years, and particularly since 2009, there has been growing remorse about Turing's 'appalling' treatment. Although the clock cannot be put back and although he was dealt with under the law of the time, on 10 September 1979 the prime minister, Gordon Brown, released a statement on behalf of the government apologising for his treatment – 'We're sorry, you deserved so much better.'

The summer of 2013 saw this taken further, with the introduction into the House of Lords of a Bill to give Turing a statutory pardon. The high-profile campaign was supported by tens of thousands of people, including Professor Stephen Hawking. As a result, in December 2013 Turing was granted a pardon by the queen under the Royal Prerogative of Mercy, a rare occurrence, usually only granted at the request of a family member:

NOW KNOW YE that We, in consideration of circumstances humbly represented to Us, are graciously pleased to extend Our Grace and Mercy unto the said Alan Mathison Turing and to grant him Our Free Pardon posthumously in respect of the said convictions;

AND to pardon and remit unto him the sentence imposed upon him as aforesaid;

AND for so doing this shall be a sufficient Warrant.

GIVEN at Our Court at [Saint James's] the [24TH] day of [December] 2013;

In the sixty-second Year of Our Reign.

By Her Majesty's Command

Turing is remembered around the world with blue plaques, statues, scholarship programmes and the naming of university buildings, lecture and computer rooms. Established in 1966, the annual Turing Award is considered to be the computing profession's equivalent to the Nobel Prize.

There have also been commemorative stamps ('Britons of Distinction'), plays, films, TV programmes, an (erroneous) assumption that his manner of death was the inspiration for the Apple computer logo (an apple with a bite taken out of it), and on the centenary of his death in 2012 even an Alan Turing edition of Monopoly.

A particularly appropriate tribute was organised in Manchester. Alan Turing was a talented long-distance runner, occasionally running the 40 miles from Bletchley to London for meetings. He was up to world-class marathon standards. On the evening of 23 June 2012, the exact centenary of his birth, the London 2012 Olympic Torch flame was passed on in front of Turing's statue in Sackville Gardens. The statue shows him seated on a bench, an apple in his hand.

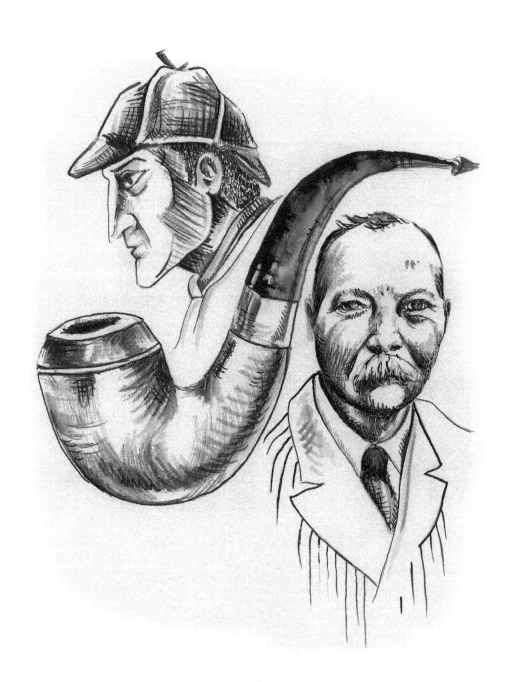

TWO LIVES

Two lives, one life,
healer, writer,
flesh and fable.

The doctor beached,
patients unseen,
but patience rewarded.

Into the study, setting the scene,
three weeks of inspiration to create
another life.
Creator and creation,
author, inquisitor,
taking their places in history

but taking the mind from better things.
Until – the hero fallen –
the writer freed.

Yet a fleeting respite,
fallen but not fallen,
slain but not slain,
the outcry heeded, the hero returns.

The writer rewarded,
for serving his king,
confounding the critics,
routing the doubters,
... the unwise war?

A change of scene, new wife, new life,
new challenger in a lost world,
new goals, new fields of play.

The sportsman ...
no longer saving goals,
no longer taking wickets,
but honing his swing.
Club Captain, a guiding light for a guiding light.

That other hero too, rewarded, retired.
Tea in the cottage on the green,
honey from the bees,
improbable, but true?

19

SIR ARTHUR CONAN DOYLE
PHYSICIAN AND WRITER

Sir Arthur Conan Doyle (1859–1930) was born in Edinburgh. He is best known as the creator of the 'consulting detective', Sherlock Holmes. Doyle had started writing short stories during his time as a medical student at the University of Edinburgh. It was to be some years, though, before he could make a living from his writing.

He was first employed as a ship's doctor on a Greenland whaler, *Hope of Peterhead*, then as ship's surgeon on *SS Mayumba* during a voyage to West Africa. 'Beached', he practised as a doctor in Plymouth (briefly), in Portsmouth (Southsea) and as an ophthalmologist in London (unsuccessfully) – he wrote in his autobiography that not a single patient had crossed his door. Consequently, in 1891 at the age of 32 he decided to abandon his medical career in favour of full-time writing.

Following the death of his first wife, Louise, from tuberculosis, he married his second wife, Jean, with whom he had maintained a platonic relationship for the last ten years of Louise's ill health. In a change of scene, they moved to Crowborough, East Sussex, in 1907, where he was to remain for the rest of his life. By then he was an established writer. In fact, by 1920 Doyle was one of the most highly paid writers in the world. His literary legacy not only includes the fifty-six short stories and four novels featuring Sherlock Holmes, but numerous other works – fantasy and science fiction, plays, romances, poetry, non-fiction and historical novels.

Since university, Doyle had been writing a series of short stories and novels but struggled to get published. Finally, following just three weeks of concentrated writing, 'patience [was] rewarded'. Sherlock Holmes (and Dr Watson) first appeared in 'A Study in Scarlet' in *Beeton's Christmas Annual* of 1887. In the poem, the other 'life', the 'fable', had appeared in 'the study', taking his 'place in history'.

Doyle's achievement of writing a complete novel in just three weeks was one of the sources of inspiration behind the National Novel Writing Month (NaNoWriMo), a challenge initiated by a group of Californian writers in 1999 and now an annual international programme. Other footsteps to follow are those of Dostoevsky, *The Gambler* (twenty-six days) and Muriel Spark, *The Prime of Miss Jean Brodie* (one month). Up to half a million aspiring writers now take part. The target is 50,000 words in the single month of November. Those who succeed receive a certificate, and some of the resulting works have become bestsellers or been made into films.

Having made the breakthrough, Doyle was on a roll. A series of sequels soon followed, published as 'The Adventures of Sherlock Holmes' in the *Strand Magazine*. In 1891, though, in one of his regular letters to his mother, (also a master storyteller), Doyle wrote 'I think of slaying Holmes ... and winding him up for good and all. He takes my mind from better things.' In particular, the 'better things' were historical novels. He wanted to be known as a 'serious' author. His mother replied, 'You won't! You can't! You mustn't!' This only gained a stay of execution, however. Two years later, in *The Final Problem*, Holmes and his adversary, Professor Moriarty, apparently plunged to their deaths together down the Reichenbach Falls in Switzerland.

However, this was to be a 'fleeting respite'. The death of Holmes sparked a public outcry. Twenty thousand readers of the *Strand Magazine* cancelled their subscriptions. Doyle heeded the outcry. In 1901, Holmes was brought back in *The Hound of the Baskervilles*, set before the Reichenbach incident. Then, two years later, after a ten-year gap, *The Return of Sherlock Holmes* signalled his reappearance in the *Strand Magazine*, again in short stories. The first of these, 'The Adventure of the Empty House', explained that only Moriarty had fallen. Holmes had faked his death to fool his other enemies.

'The writer rewarded' refers to Doyle's knighthood, granted by King Edward VII in 1902. Following service as a volunteer doctor in a field hospital in the Boer War, Doyle had written a short work justifying Britain's role in the conflict. Although he believed this was the reason for his honour, it was also well known that the king was a great Sherlock Holmes fan and would have been delighted at his reappearance!

The 'change of scene, new wife, new life', upon his move to Crowborough, also saw the creation of a second popular fictional character. The 1912 novel, *The Lost World*, introduced Professor George Edward Challenger. A gift for film-makers, film versions have been produced in 1925, 1960, 1992 and 1998.

'The sportsman ...' refers to another lesser-known talent of Doyle. Since his school days at Stoneyhurst College he had been an all-round sportsman. While in Southsea he had been goalkeeper for Portsmouth AFC (an amateur side) under the pseudonym A.C. Smith. Upon moving to London, between 1899 and 1907 he played ten first-class matches for the MCC (Marylebone Cricket Club), upon one occasion taking the wicket of W.G. Grace.

Now in Sussex and living at Windlesham, near Crowborough Beacon Golf Club, he honed his passion for golf, becoming club captain in 1910 – 'A guiding light for a guiding light'. One of his golfing companions there was Rudyard Kipling, who also lived nearby and whom he had infected with the golfing bug when he visited Kipling's house in Vermont. He took his clubs, gave Kipling a lesson, and passed on the affliction.

The final verse returns to 'that other hero', Sherlock Holmes, in his retirement to 'a small farm on the Sussex Downs, five miles from Eastbourne' (preface to *His Last Bow*, 1917). In the village of East Dean, identified by several Sherlock Holmes fans as the likely location, there is an old flint cottage on the green, opposite the popular Tiger Inn, with a blue plaque. The inscription reads 'SHERLOCK HOLMES Consulting Detective & Bee Keeper retired here 1903–1917'.

There is a memorial statue of Sir Arthur Conan Doyle in Crowborough and of Holmes in Edinburgh, Baker Street (London) and even in the UK Embassy in Moscow, installed following a Soviet TV series. Like Doyle, the fictional Holmes was also 'rewarded'. In 2002, the Royal Society of Chemistry bestowed an honorary fellowship upon him for his use of forensic science and analytical chemistry in popular literature. No wonder that in a survey of 1,000 Britons by the search engine 'Ask Jeeves', 21 per cent of respondents believed that Sherlock Holmes really existed.

After all, as Holmes would have said, 'When you have eliminated the impossible, whatever remains, however improbable, must be the truth.' (*The Sign of Four*, Sir Arthur Conan Doyle, 1890, Chapter 6.)

VISION

From Scottish shore to Sussex shore,
Inventor, not conqueror,
but no less invading our lives.

The time had come to talk of many things,
from hatbox, needles, cycle lights,
from sealing wax and glue,
an image through the looking glass
the future came in view.

Shocked landlord of a shocked survivor.
Asked to leave.
Resettled in a Soho room,
a change of place, a change of pace.

A flying spot scanned Stooky Bill.
The dummy run repeated –
claims accepted,
doubts resolved,
the sceptics now defeated?

New voices heard, new views take hold,
as fanned by flames, by molten glass,
new science takes shape, rejecting old.

Transmitted now across the seas,
His colours won, grey days no more,
One thousand lines at end of war –
too much, too soon, plans put on hold.

Patents filed, seeds sown,
But sixty years to grow.
His wartime projects saving lives,
But sadly not his own.

Returned to Sussex shore,
no fortune but his legacy,
and that worth so much more.

20

JOHN LOGIE BAIRD
INVENTOR AND TELEVISION PIONEER

The poem this time is a bit uncomfortable to read. Some verses rhyme and read smoothly, others do not. This is deliberate. The idea was to reflect the flickering images, uncomfortable to watch, of the first mechanical television, and the stop-start nature of later developments. Smooth progress was punctuated by step changes in technology and interrupted by the Second World War.

John Logie Baird was born in Helensburgh, then in the county of Dunbartonshire, on 14 August 1888, and died in Bexhill, Sussex, on 14 June 1946. Although rightly regarded as one of the greatest Scottish scientists, his initial pioneering work on television was carried out in Sussex.

The poem title, 'Vision', refers to both Baird's inspiration, his vision of the future, and to our sense of sight, as in the word 'television'.

In 1923 (aged 34) after suffering a health breakdown, he had moved to 21 Linton Crescent, Hastings. It was there that he built the world's first working TV set, his very first transmitted image being a Maltese cross. As his work continued he needed more space and so rented a workshop in Queen's Arcade. Both buildings now mark his pioneering work with commemorative plaques.

That first set looked nothing like the TV sets we know today, being semi-mechanical, and of course he had to improvise the components. These included 'an old hatbox, a pair of scissors, some darning needles, a few bicycle light lenses (four pence each), a used tea chest, sealing wax and glue'. It was powered by a small electric fan motor. When writing the poem, I'm afraid that the parallels with Lewis Carroll's 'The Walrus and the Carpenter' in *Through the Looking Glass and What Alice Found There*, were too hard to resist:

> 'The time has come,' the Walrus said,
> 'To talk of many things:
> Of shoes ... and ships ... and sealing-wax ...
> Of cabbages ... and kings ...
> And why the sea is boiling hot ...
> And whether pigs have wings.'

Baird also thought that 'the time had come ...' to crack the problems that had defeated other inventors. Both included 'sealing wax' among their requisites, and of course Baird invented the ultimate 'looking glass'.

Within the year he was able to successfully demonstrate his invention to the *Radio Times*. His experiments continued, but not without incident. After surviving a 1,000-volt electric shock, his landlord must have decided that he was a bit of a fire risk and asked him to leave. He relocated his laboratory to Soho, made a technical breakthrough, and on 2 October 1925 transmitted the famous first greyscale television picture of the head of a ventriloquist's dummy, 'Stooky Bill'.

He had used a 'flying spot' scanning technique. The demonstration was repeated on 26 January 1926 before an invited, but somewhat sceptical, audience of around fifty scientists and Royal Institution members. Baird, with an eye to publicity, had also invited a reporter from *The Times*. The event was a success and was the world's first public demonstration of 'real' television with live moving images and tone graduation. Quoted in *The Times* two days later, Baird admitted that he had been on edge, 'would they admit that a wretched nonentity* working with soap boxes in a garret had done something which many of them had stated was not possible?' (*Baird's degree course at Glasgow University had been interrupted by the First World War and so he never completed his degree.)

Although his visitors had somewhat grudgingly accepted the claims he made for his 'Televisor', there was a reservation – 'It has yet to be seen to what extent further developments will carry Mr Baird's system towards practical use.'

Over the next few years Baird made rapid progress, full tone graduation, moving images and by 1928 the first transatlantic TV transmission, colour transmission and stereoscopic TV (the forerunner of 3D TV). In 1931 he televised the first live transmission of the Epsom Derby, the beginnings of 'outside broadcasting'. By 1938 he had developed a large screen (15ft by 12ft) colour theatre projection system to bring a live boxing match to an audience of 3,000 in the Dominium Theatre – another first.

However, new technology had overtaken his semi-mechanical system. Cathode ray tube systems had finally become viable. In 1937, following comparative trials, the BBC went over to Marconi-EMI's newly developed electronic system, based on an American (RCA) system.

In the poem, the line 'fanned by flames, by molten glass' refers to an event which probably didn't help Baird's case. A disastrous fire on 30 November 1936 burnt the Crystal Palace to the ground. Watched by an estimated 100,000 people, among them Winston Churchill, one theory was that the fire had been started by an electrical fault due to old wiring in the extensive Baird Television Complex. Unknown to most people at the time, this largest broadcasting facility in Europe had been constructed right underneath the main concourse. Joseph Paxton's iconic landmark, built to house the Great Exhibition of 1851, may have been the first victim of a television equipment overnight fire – what a reminder to switch the set off!

Baird himself switched to electronic systems. He developed his 1920s 'flying spot' scanning method for cathode ray tubes (still in use), further developed his early form of HDTV 3D colour television, and in 1943 proposed a national

1,000 line HDTV system to the Hankey Committee – this was a government taskforce set up to examine the future of television.

He also proposed that most television programmes be pre-recorded (he had also invented a video recorder). Today, 95 per cent of TV programmes are in fact produced in this way. His ideas were turned down. There were higher priorities at the end of the war, and lesser standards were adopted.

In failing health, Baird returned to 'the fresh air and dry climate' of the Sussex coast, to a semi-detached house in Station Road, Bexhill. The house was chosen so that he could continue to commute to his laboratory, but possibly he no longer had the stamina to fight his corner. He died in 1946, less than two years later.

Little is known about his top secret work for the government in the Second World War, but it is claimed that he contributed to the development of radar, signal jamming and mine detectors – as used at El Alamein and the D-Day landings.

Between 1923 and the late 1930s he had filed 178 patents, and sown the seeds for most of the subsequent developments in television. His 1928 techniques were used for Neil Armstrong's first colour transmissions from the moon. The 405-line TV standard wasn't upgraded to 625 lines until 1964 and we have only enjoyed his HDTV 3D standards in the last few years. Colour (PAL) transmissions took until 1967, and over sixty years after his large screen Dominion Theatre transmission, the BBC reported on 'a demonstration of large screen three-dimensional television'.

All this despite the fact that, in the early 1930s, in the time of Lord Reith, the first Director General of the BBC, the corporation had been extremely reluctant to introduce a regular television service. The historian Asa Briggs believed that Lord Reith, the son of a minister of the Free Church of Scotland, saw television as a threat to society – 'He thought it would really corrupt and ruin the nation'.

Baird never made any money out of his work, financing most of his research out of his own pocket. At the end of the 1920s he could have sold his company for a fortune but it was said that he would have had no idea of what to do with the money. 'A laboratory with all the apparatus I wanted was to me a perfect paradise ... the perfect place from which to see the future' (John Logie Baird, from the documentary, *JLB – the Man who saw the Future*).

Baird's rented house in Bexhill was demolished in 2007 and the area replaced with the Egerton Place development. This includes a new block of flats named Baird Court.

COR CORDIUM

A birthright rejected, a driven soul, a final storm.
Childhood days, happy days, fishing, hunting, walks in the moonlight.
Change ... too soon from Sussex fields to playing fields
of Eton. The dreamer displaced, friendless, tormented.
Change ... onwards and upwards, the well-worn path
to Oxford. Writer, radical, rebel,
polemic in a paper boat, a step too far,
expelled.

A flight, a teenage marriage. Failed.
His wife, his child, abandoned for another.
A flight once more, a continental tour. Cut short.
To Mary a daughter, to Mary a son.
Abroad again, on Lake Geneva's shores, ghosts, stories,
To Mary ... a monster.

Travellers. Florence, Pisa, Rome.
And writing. Poems epic, poems lyric,
poems of protest, poems of love,
elegies and tragedies,
and tragedies their own.

Death of a sister, death of a wife,
death of a daughter, death of a son.
'Alas I have nor hope nor health
Nor peace within nor calm around.'

A reckless journey, the final storm,
Ariel lost beneath the waves.
Ten miles to sea, ten days to shore,
no hands, no face. Known by
the poems in his pocket. Known by
the clothes that he wore.

Ariel's song adorns his grave.
Ashes in Rome, his heart brought home. Reunited,
in Mary's tomb, *'Why not I with thine?'*

A tragic life, a tragic death, but sowing seeds.
Writers, reformers, composers, performers –
the harvesters, heirs to his vision,
The Triumph of Life.

21

PERCY BYSSHE SHELLEY
ENGLISH ROMANTIC POET

The poem title, the Latin phrase *'cor cordium'* ('heart of hearts') appears on Shelley's gravestone in the Protestant Cemetery in Rome (Campo Cestio). The cemetery is also known as the Cemetery of Poets. His friend John Keats is also buried there. The burial of Shelley's ashes in that ground, with that inscription, is doubly ironic. Firstly, he was a lifelong atheist, and secondly, his actual heart was removed from his funeral pyre and taken back to England.

Percy Bysshe Shelley was born on 4 August 1792 in Field Place, in the parish of Warnham, about 1 mile north-east of the village of Broadbridge Heath on the outskirts of Horsham, West Sussex. Field Place is now a grade one listed building, the earliest parts dating back to the fifteenth century.

Shelley was baptised on 7 September 1792 in Warnham Church and up to the age of 10 enjoyed an idyllic childhood in the local Sussex countryside. In his book, *There's More Here Than You Think – A Detailed History of Broadbridge Heath*, local resident Jonathan England mentions the young Shelley's 'walks in the moonlight' to visit his grandfather at Arun House in Horsham. He is said to have sheltered in a Broadbridge Heath barn on at least one occasion. Perhaps he got caught in a storm or the moon didn't sufficiently light his way? The barn later (1905) became the first clubhouse for Horsham Golf Club's original nine-hole layout (the club relocated to Mannings Heath in 1914). The opening line of the poem gives a nine-word summary of what was to come, his life and tragic early death.

Percy was the eldest of six children, the heir of Sir Timothy Shelley MP and his landowning wife, Elizabeth (Pilford). His grandfather was a baronet and his uncle was a famous naval commander who served under Admiral Nelson during the Battle of Trafalgar. He was born into privilege and prosperity, what Ana Sampson termed 'solid, conservative aristocratic stock'. But it was 'a birthright rejected'. He was to shock Regency England with his revolutionary political idealism.

Sent away firstly to school at Syon House Academy in Brentford, Middlesex, he was prepared for his entry to Eton College in 1804. Although academically he succeeded in gaining entrance to University College Oxford, socially Eton was a disaster. Shelley was a quiet, rather eccentric character, shoelaces undone, a bit of a daydreamer, always with his nose in a book, a bit of a 'swot'. He already had strong views on respect for the rights of others and would not take part in 'fagging'. Coupled with his indifference to sport and other youthful activities, this set him apart. He was nicknamed 'Mad Shelley' and suffered almost daily taunting, 'Shelley-baiting', by the other boys. He lashed out, ineffectually, at his tormentors and of course this just made things worse. He made no friends at Eton.

He trod 'the well-worn path to Oxford' in 1810. He rarely attended lectures, but read and wrote constantly. In the course of one year he published two Gothic novels and two poetry collections, including works by others as well as his own pieces. University College had a strong Christian tradition and so his next pamphlet, *The Necessity of Atheism*, led to his expulsion. 'Polemic in a paper boat' was, in truth, a post-expulsion development. Shelley adopted some very odd ways to distribute his flow of political pamphlets, sending them out in paper boats or bottles on waterways or inside hot-air balloons.

Verse 2 concerns Shelley's two marriages; in both cases he took up with 16-year-olds. Soon after being sent down from Oxford at the age of 19, he eloped to Scotland and married Harriet Westbrook, a school friend of his sister. Harriet bore him two children, but the marriage failed. Harriet was not his intellectual equal. Three years after his marriage to Harriet, he became besotted with Mary Godwin. Mary was the highly educated daughter of two intellectual heavyweights. Her father, and Shelley's mentor at the time, was the like-minded social reformer William Godwin and her mother was the feminist Mary Wollstonecraft. Mary Godwin was someone he could talk to.

The flight this time was to the continent, through France to Switzerland, in the company of Mary's stepsister, Claire Clairmont. Claire could speak French. Like later young Interrailers, after six weeks they had had enough. They had run out of money, they were homesick and Mary was pregnant. Their daughter was born in February 1815, but only lived for a few weeks. Within a few months Mary was pregnant again. This time their son, William, survived through infancy.

'Abroad again', Mary, Shelley and Claire spent the summer of 1816 at Lake Geneva. Shelley's poetry writing had by now received some acclaim. An early influence had been Wordsworth (1770–1850) and he was now to meet with the self-exiled Lord Byron. The two men rented nearby houses on the lake.

One evening, at Byron's place, he invited his guests to take part in a 'ghost story contest'. Mary, then 18 years old, mulled this over for several days before coming up with the idea of a young science student who, by means of a very unorthodox experiment, creates a living creature from the body parts of the dead, only to be horrified by the monster he had created. Two years later, *Frankenstein* was published. It is not recorded whether Mary won the contest!

Early in 1818 the Shelleys took to the road again, this time in Italy, leaving England for good – 'Travellers. Florence, Pisa, Rome'. Travelling, writing and meeting fellow poets, Shelley's output was by now wide ranging and immense. His best-known short poem, a sonnet, *Ozymandias of Egypt*, written before their departure, also featured a traveller – 'I met a traveller from an antique land …' It was, however, during their own travels that one of Shelley's best-known longer works was written. This was the elegy *Adonais*, fifty-five nine-line verses inspired by the death of his friend, John Keats.

Before and during these years, though, there had been 'tragedies of their own'. Mary's other half-sister, Fanny Imlay, had killed herself in Wales in early October 1816. Two months later Shelley's first, estranged, wife Harriet drowned herself in the Serpentine in Hyde Park, pregnant by her new lover. This did of course enable Shelley and Mary to then marry. 'Death of a daughter' was of their baby daughter Clara, born in 1817 in England, who died in Italy in 1818. After Clara's death, Shelley, in failing health and with a disintegrating marriage, had composed *Stanzas written in Dejection, near Naples*, the opening two lines of which are quoted as the final two lines of Verse 4. As if that was not enough, their 3-year-old son William then also became ill and died the following year.

Shelley wrote about love and death with great compassion. A gem of only eight lines, but which quietly encapsulates such deep feelings is *Music, When Soft Voices Die*:

> Music, when soft voices die,
> Vibrates in the memory –
> Odours, when sweet violets sicken,
> Live within the sense they quicken.

> Rose leaves, when the rose is dead,
> Are heaped for the beloved's bed;
> And so thy thoughts, when thou art gone,
> Love itself shall slumber on.

In 1822, Shelley invited the poet and editor Leigh Hunt and his family to join them on the Gulf of Spezia, on the Ligurian coast, a part of what is now more commonly known as the Italian Riviera (northern Italy). The Shelleys, Mary's stepsister Claire and some friends, Edward and Jane Williams, were staying in a rented house, right on the edge of the sea, in Lerici. Back then it was a wild and remote area. Shelley was inspired, and began to write what was to become his last, unfinished, poem – *The Triumph of Life*.

Mary hated the place. She had already lost three of her four children and was pregnant again. On 16 June Mary suffered a severe miscarriage. Following this, she was prone to violent mood swings and was convinced that some tragedy was about to befall them. Shelley himself was also suffering from violent nightmares and strange visions.

However, Shelley was set on advancing a political periodical publishing project, also involving Lord Byron, the setting up of which was the reason why Leigh Hunt had been invited to join them. This required sailing his new boat, with Edward Williams as crew, on a long trip down the coast to Livorno. The new boat had been especially built for Shelley's sailing holiday, but he was no boat designer. He had had extra top masts and sails fitted so that he could outpace Byron's new boat, the *Bolivar*, when racing in the bay. There was considerable, but friendly, rivalry. Shelley had even rejected Byron's original suggested name for his new boat – *Don Juan* became *Ariel*.

A week later, on 8 July 1822, his business completed, they set sail for home, this time taking an 18-year-old boat boy too as an extra pair of hands. A storm blew up but Shelley pressed on, carrying a reckless amount of sail for such high winds and heavy seas. At one stage they were even approached by another concerned skipper who offered to take the inexperienced trio aboard his own boat and out of danger.

Shelley refused; he didn't want to lose his boat. Instead he pressed on ... and lost his life. *Ariel* capsized 10 miles offshore. Shelley and his companions all drowned. Shelley was just 29 years of age. Mary's forebodings had been realised. Ten days later his body was washed ashore. His hands and face had been eaten away. He was identified only by a book of his friend Keats' poems in his pocket, and by his clothes.

In accordance with the Italian quarantine laws in force at the time to guard against plague, his body was first buried in the sand where he had been found. But then a month later it was dug up again and burnt on a pyre on the same beach in the presence of Lord Byron, Leigh Hunt and another friend, Edward Trelawney. With great presence of mind, Trelawney retrieved Shelley's charred heart from the fire.

By a circuitous route it was returned to Mary, and after she died was placed with her own remains and those of her parents in the Shelley family tomb in St Peter's Church, Bournemouth. Shelley's heart was said to have been discovered pressed between the pages of a copy of *Adonais*. Some years later, the bodies of her surviving son Percy and his wife were also to join them in the family tomb. The quote, 'Why not I with thine?' is from Shelley's poem, *Love's Philosophy*. I will admit to having used this out of context, but no more so than the same poem's use in the two TV series, *Twin Peaks* and *Lewis* (Series 2).

There is a very fine combined memorial to Shelley and Mary in Christchurch Priory, not far away from their tomb in St Peter's Church. This contains a complete nine-line verse from *Adonais* which starts, 'He has outsoared the shadow of our night' (Verse XL).

I started this explanation with an inscription on Shelley's gravestone in Rome, where lie his ashes. The phrase '*cor cordium*' ('heart of hearts') was suggested by his friend and fellow romantic poet, Leigh Hunt. There is another text on the stone, indicated by the line 'Ariel's song adorns his grave'. The extract is from 'Ariel's Song', in Shakespeare's *The Tempest* (Act I):

Nothing of him that doth fade
But doth suffer a sea-change
Into something rich and strange.

This was suggested by Edward Trelawney, as *The Tempest* was Shelley's favourite play and the text was thought particularly appropriate in view of the manner of Shelley's death. Both men had been present on the beach when his disfigured body had been dug up and his heart rescued from the subsequent funeral pyre.

The final verse of the poem highlights Shelley's legacy, 'sowing seeds'. 'The harvesters, heirs to his vision' are many and varied. The writers his works have influenced include the next three generations of poets, among them Robert Browning, Alfred Lord Tennyson, Dante Gabriel Rossetti, Algernon Charles Swinburne, Thomas Hardy and the Indian poet, Rabindranath Tagore. It was not only poets who fell under his spell. Other admirers included George Bernard Shaw, Bertrand Russell, Henry David Thoreau and C.S. Lewis. The reformers included the Chartists, Karl Marx, Leo Tolstoy and Mahatma Gandhi. Besides writers, the composers Sergei Rachmaninov and Samuel Barber paid homage.

As well as the directors of the previously mentioned TV series and other dramatists, a performer particularly in tune with Shelley's ideals was the free-spirited American modern dancer Isadora Duncan, famous in the early 1920s. Shelley was one of the poets whose works were read to 'Clan Duncan' by their mother from an early age. Isadora grew up sharing Shelley's beliefs in atheism, free love and the value of Grecian culture, and was one of the first feminists – shades of Mary Shelley's mother. Her dance was once described as 'poetry personified'.

Shelley's life would appear to have been a catalogue of disasters, but as another famous Sussex poet put it:

> If you can meet with Triumph and Disaster
> And treat those two imposters just the same;
> [...]
> Yours is the Earth and everything that's in it,
> [...]
>
> (*If*, Rudyard Kipling.)

Shelley's greatest 'triumph' is in his lasting influence. His vision is as much a source of inspiration today as it has been across the almost 200 years since his death. What better way, then, than to borrow as my last line the title of Shelley's own last unfinished poem – *The Triumph of Life*.

REVOLUTIONARY

Bowls on the Castle Green, skating on the ponds,
debating at the White Hart Inn,
headstrong and restless. Across the larger pond
the colonies, inspired, broke free.
Across the Channel, the fight for liberty.
The places that shaped him.

Staymaker – briefly,
exciseman – absently,
shopkeeper – fallibly, but
a writer of genius, his pen his sword.
Visionary, revolutionary,
campaigner, reformer.
Great Briton, French citizen,
conscience of the world.
The roles that defined him.

Franklin, Washington,
Jefferson, Lincoln –
friends and supporters.
Robespierre, Roosevelt –
foes and detractors.
The people who heard him.

Tyranny, poverty, bribery, sleaze.
Drive out the old, ring in the new,
the rule of law, the rights of man,
the common sense for common good.
Government of the people by
the people – freedom, reason, trust.
Tell it to the future world –
begin the world again. Imagine.
The causes that drove him.

No heroes burial, no pomp,
no pageantry, no gratitude.
Denounced, despised, forgotten.
His body snatched. Best intent, but
scattered bones, yet his unfading voice
still echoes. His words still speak to us,
inspire, endure.
The words that redeemed him.

22

THOMAS PAINE

INFLUENTIAL WRITER AND CHAMPION OF THE RIGHTS OF MAN

Thomas Paine was born in Thetford, Norfolk, on 9 February 1737. Before coming to Lewes, East Sussex, at the age of 31, he had worked at a variety of jobs in Norfolk, Kent, Lincolnshire, Cornwall and London. As a teenager, he had even spent a short time at sea as a privateer.

It was during his time living at Bull House (1768–74) that he first really involved himself in politics and employed his talent for the telling phrase. Since the seventeenth century Lewes had had a tradition of opposition to the monarchy, instead favouring republicanism. He felt at home. Paine was a leading member of the Headstrong Club, a political debating club which met at the White Hart Inn.

Paine had always been a restless soul, though, and following his move to London in 1774 he was soon off again. This time it was to British colonial America, specifically Pennsylvania, armed with a letter of recommendation from Benjamin Franklin to whom he had been introduced in London. He wrote the pamphlet *Common Sense*, which was published anonymously ('Written by an Englishman') in January 1776, after the revolution had started. It spread like wildfire and cemented the idea of separation from Britain among the general public and paved the way for the *Declaration of Independence* (4 July 1776). His arguments were clear, concise and written in the language of the common man – 'A long habit of not thinking a thing wrong gives it a superficial appearance of being right.' At a critical point in the war George Washington ordered Paine's pamphlet, *The American Crisis. Number 1*, to be read to all the troops at Valley Forge:

> These are the times that try men's souls: The summer soldier and the sunshine patriot will, in this crisis, shrink from the service of their country; but he that stands it now, deserves the love and thanks of man and woman. Tyranny, like Hell, is not easily conquered; yet we have this consolation with us, that the harder the conflict, the more glorious the triumph. What we obtain too cheap, we esteem too lightly: it is dearness only that gives everything its value …

The army had been on the verge of disintegration. It saved the day. The effect would have been similar to King Henry V's famous speech before Harfleur in Shakespeare's play:

Once more unto the breach, dear friends, once more;
Or close the wall up with our English dead!
In peace there is nothing so becomes a man
As modest stillness and humility:
But when the blast of war blows in our ears,
Then imitate the action of the tiger;
[...]
Follow your spirit; and, upon this charge
Cry 'God for Harry! England and Saint George!'

Throughout his life, the quality that marked Paine out from his contemporaries was his writing – 'a writer of genius'. 'His pen his sword' condenses a quote attributed to John Adams, George Washington's vice president and successor as president, 'Without the pen of Paine, the sword of Washington would have been wielded in vain'. The essence of this tribute is also to be found on plaques on both the White Hart Hotel and Bull House, in Lewes High Street.

However, one successful revolution was not enough for Paine. As he later said, to play a part in two revolutions was to live to some purpose. His next stop was France. The French Revolution was under way. His departure was a matter of expediency, as his next publication, *The Rights of Man* (1791), tore into the institution of monarchy and aristocracy – 'two ancient tyrannies'. Coming on top of *Common Sense*, which had led to the loss of the colonies, King George III was not happy.

Paine takes a hearty swipe at monarchy in general, and Britain's system of government in particular. He didn't confine himself to criticism of the British monarchy, though, he also voiced his concerns about the French monarchy's possible territorial ambitions in no uncertain terms, 'A French bastard landing with armed banditti and establishing himself King of England, against the consent of the natives, is, in plain terms, a very paltry, rascally original. It certainly has no divinity in it.'

Paine didn't confine his views to any one country. He was in favour of a democratic application of the law to support the 'Rights of Man' globally, 'For as in absolute governments the king is law, so in free countries the law ought to be king; and there ought to be no other'. Paine espoused the ideals of the French Revolution and so had gone to France to support it.

In truth, the authorities had chased him out of Britain and in his absence he was convicted of seditious libel, which carried a death sentence. Unsurprisingly, he never returned to England. In contrast, the new French Revolutionary government granted him honorary French citizenship. All was not well, though, between the two warring factions within the French Revolutionary government. Paine found himself on the wrong side, was arrested, imprisoned and narrowly escaped the guillotine. With the fall of Robespierre he was reinstated and lived in Paris until 1802, at which time he returned to the United States at President Jefferson's invitation.

Paine, however, contrived to make more enemies, particularly in America, with the publication of *The Age of Reason*. This was a theological work which challenged institutionalised religion and the legitimacy of the Bible. It was written in his customary no-punches-pulled style, 'The story of Eve and the serpent, and of Noah and his ark, drops to a level with the Arabian tales, without the merit of being entertaining'.

This did not go down well in the primarily Christian society of the America of the time, or indeed for some time after his death. Theodore Roosevelt (president from 1901 to 1909) referred to him as that 'filthy little atheist'. He was, though, perhaps the victim of knee-jerk reactions. He remained a believer in 'one God, and no more; and I hope for happiness beyond this life'. His criticism was of competing religious sects and the uncritical belief in what he called the 'mythology' of the Bible – 'My own mind is my own church'.

The publication of *The Age of Reason* was a bolt from the blue. Up until then Paine had been the 'Conscience of the world'. In various works he had advocated the abolition of slavery, the emancipation of women, government measures to fight poverty, and private ownership of property. *The Rights of Man*, published in 1791, had been a runaway bestseller. Paine maintained that the sole purpose of government was to safeguard the family and their rights. He was generations ahead of his time. He proposed many of the reforms that we now take for granted: state pensions, welfare benefits financed out of taxation, a minimum wage and better working conditions, freedom of information and the right to vote to be determined by age rather than property ownership. It was a Utopian image.

These ideals are reflected in 'the causes that drove him'. The verse includes the titles of two of his best-known works, *The Rights of Man* and *Common Sense*. 'Government of the people by the people', a central theme of Paine's, is a quote from the end of Abraham Lincoln's *Gettysburg Address* (19 November 1863, at the time of the American Civil War).

'Tell it to the future world …' brings us into the present. President Barack Obama quoted directly from Paine's *The American Crisis No. 1* in his inauguration speech. Indeed, CNN News reported, 'if the speech could be said to have an animating spirit, it was that of Thomas Paine'. Paine's belief, expressed in *Common Sense*, that 'We have it in our power to begin the world over again', was echoed in the president's message.

'Imagine' captures this same feeling in John Lennon's bestselling song. In a 1980 interview, asked about its underlying meaning, he answered, 'If you can imagine a world at peace, with no denomination of religion – not without religion but without this my-God-is-bigger-than-your-God thing – then it can be true'.

In another age and phraseology this could have been an exact quote from Paine's controversial later work, *The Age of Reason*. Lennon's lines, with only a minor change (bracketed) – 'You may say [he's] a dreamer, but [he's] not the only one', could indeed refer to Thomas Paine. A cover of 'Imagine', by Emeli Sande, was used by the BBC at the close of the 2012 Summer Olympics, striking a chord worldwide.

The final verse tells of the final chapter of Paine's story. His last years were spent in poverty, often depressed, the worse for drink and in poor health. He died in Greenwich Village, New York City, on 8 June 1809, aged 72. In 1784 he had been given a 320-acre farm by the New York State Legislature for his services in the American Revolution. It was in New Rochelle, New York State. Denied a burial in the Quaker graveyard, as he had requested, he was buried under a walnut tree in a corner of his farm. The *New York Evening Post* obituary read, 'He had lived long, did some good, and much harm'. Only six mourners came to his funeral. The good was largely forgotten:

> Thomas Paine had passed the legendary limit of life. One by one most of his old friends and acquaintances had deserted him. Maligned on every side, execrated, shunned and abhorred – his virtues denounced as vices – his services forgotten – his character blackened, he preserved the poise and balance of his soul. He was a victim of the people, but his convictions remained unshaken. He was still a soldier in the army of freedom, and still tried to enlighten and civilise those who were impatiently waiting for his death. Even those who loved their enemies hated him, their friend – the friend of the whole world – with all their hearts. On the 8th of June, 1809, death came – Death, almost his only friend. At his funeral no pomp, no pageantry, no civic procession, no military display. In a carriage, a woman and her son who had lived on the bounty of the dead – on horseback, a Quaker, the humanity of whose heart dominated the creed of his head – and, following on foot, two Negroes filled with gratitude – constituted the funeral cortege of Thomas Paine.
>
> (Paine's obituary, Robert G. Ingersoll, *New York Evening Post*, 10 June 1809.)

Ten years later, the English radical politician and writer, William Cobbett, dug up his remains and 'repatriated' them to England. Cobbett had wished to honour his mentor. Cobbett's grand plans for a memorial, however, never materialised and the boxed bones were passed down to his eldest son, William, who went bankrupt in 1836. The bones were sold off and the story is that these have become scattered all over the world. This has become 'the stuff of legends', there is even a present-day song by Graham Moore entitled 'Tom Paine's Bones'. Ironically, if the story is true, in death Paine has truly fulfilled his claim that 'My country is the world'.

Paine influenced many like minds, among them Bertrand Russell, and his plan for a welfare state underpinned the British Beveridge Report of 1942. In a 2002 public poll by the BBC, Paine was voted 34th of the '100 Greatest Britons'. Paine is now also regarded as one of the fathers of the American Revolution and the founding of the United States of America.

Although not exactly 'a statue of gold erected to you in every city in the universe' that his contemporary Napoleon Bonaparte had proposed, there are memorials to Paine in New Rochelle, New Jersey, Thetford, Lewes and Paris. As the poem's final line recognises, his words have redeemed him.

ENDURANCE

Eight years before the mast,
master mariner, explorer,
hero in an age of heroes.

A leader of a different type,
small wages, bitter cold,
darkness, danger, doubts –
but a man to bring us safe
through triumph or disaster.

In British waters – war.
In Polar seas, another foe,
The stirring ice, the giant below.
Endurance trapped, a lethal vice,
a broken hull, the giant's price.

Endurance tested.
The open boat,
six men against the storms,
against the odds.
His men – stranded, rescued, returned.
They never doubted.

The Boss,
inspired, inspiring,
'spouting lines from Keats',
lines by heart,
but a heart that failed.

Now written in stone,
A line to remember a life.
A name to live in the minds of men,
ships, boats, trains and planes,
a crater on the moon. Legacy,
a name that lives in history.

23

SIR ERNEST SHACKLETON
POLAR EXPLORER AND
LEADERSHIP ROLE MODEL

Sir Ernest Shackleton (1874–1922) and his wife Emily (*née* Dorman, 1868–1936) lived at 14 Milnthorpe Road, Meads, Eastbourne, from 1916 to 1922, the year of his death at the age of 47 in South Georgia on his last expedition. Emily lived on at the house for some years before moving to Coldwaltham, West Sussex, where she and their unmarried daughter, Cicely, are buried. Their joint gravestone can be found in St Giles churchyard.

Another Sussex connection is that Emily's father, Charles Dorman, was 'of Towngate Farm, Wadhurst, Sussex', although Emily was born and later met Ernest Shackleton after the family had moved to Sydenham, south London. The two families lived only a short distance apart. Emily, six years older than Ernest, was a friend of Ernest's sister, which is how they first met in 1897. They were married in 1904 following a courtship interrupted by Shackleton's absences at sea.

In November 1994, Eastbourne Borough Council, following a suggestion by the Eastbourne (Civic) Society, erected a blue plaque at 14 Milnthorpe Road, marking Shackleton's last years there – when not on expeditions! In a letter, Shackleton wrote that it was 'the dearest little house' that he had ever lived in.

Having left Dulwich College at the age of 16, 'I never learned much geography at school', he served an eight-year apprenticeship to gain a Master Mariner Certificate, starting on the square-rigged sailing ship *Houghton Tower*. This qualified him to command a British Merchant Navy ship anywhere in the world.

It was during these-years at sea that he learnt to be at ease with all kinds of men. In his first Antarctic expedition (*Discovery*, 1901–03), led by Captain Robert Scott, he was described as 'the most popular of the officers among the crew, being a good mixer'. On the return journey of his own second expedition (*Nimrod*, 1907–09), racing against starvation, he gave his one daily biscuit to an ailing companion, who wrote in his diary 'the remembrance of that sacrifice will never leave me'. At that time, he and three companions had made the largest advance to the pole in exploration history. On his return home he was knighted by King Edward VII.

After the miraculous rescue of his men on his third expedition, the ill-fated Imperial Trans-Antarctic Expedition (*Endurance*, 1914–17), and already a 'hero in an age of heroes', one of Captain Scott's team wrote, 'If I am in the devil of a hole and want to get out of it, give me Shackleton every time'. In the poem, this is expressed as 'a man to bring us safe through triumph or disaster'. This also echoes a line from his contemporary, Rudyard Kipling's well-known poem *If* – 'If you can meet with Triumph and Disaster, And treat those two imposters just the same'.

Shackleton's outstanding leadership qualities are still used as a role model in corporate management courses today. He was 'a leader of a different type'. The next lines in the poem quote from a famous, but perhaps mythical, advertisement for men to join the *Endurance* Expedition:

> Men wanted: For Hazardous journey. Small wages, bitter cold, long months of complete darkness, constant danger, safe return doubtful. Honour and recognition in case of success. – Ernest Shackleton.

Whether this was really the way that he announced the expedition or not, as his requirement was made public:

> The first result of this was a flood of applications from all classes of the community to join the adventure. I received nearly five thousand applications, and out of these were picked fifty-six men. (Preface to *South: The Endurance Expedition*, Sir Ernest Shackleton.)

The men were outnumbered by the sleigh dogs. There were seventy and they all had names. These included Songster, Mercury, Hercules, Spotty, Slobbers, Sooty, Sweep, Splitlip, Satan, Painfull, Fluffy, Smuts and Shakespeare. Someone must have had great fun naming the dogs!

Despite the outbreak of the First World War on 3 August 1914, *Endurance* was directed by Winston Churchill, then First Lord of the Admiralty, to 'proceed'. The ship left British waters five days later. In the play *Shackleton's Carpenter*, the *Endurance* is described as stopping overnight at Eastbourne Pier on 4 August 1914 where they were 'warmly welcomed by thousands. The ship continued to Plymouth on August 5th, from where it sailed to Buenos Aires and the Antarctic.'

'In Polar seas, another foe,/The stirring ice, the giant below' – in the poem the second line is extracted from a longer quote from Shackleton's description of the fate of the *Endurance*. Trapped in pack ice over the Antarctic winter and spring she was slowly crushed – 'Endurance trapped, a lethal vice,/ a broken hull, the giant's price'.

The crew had to abandon the sinking ship and camp on the sea ice. Realising they would not be found, they launched their three lifeboats and sailed the 346 miles to Elephant Island. However, this was also not on any trade routes. Shackleton then selected the strongest boat, which the ship's carpenter, Harry McNish, further toughened up for a seemingly impossible 720 nautical-mile stormy ocean voyage, at times through hurricane force winds, to the inhabited island of South Georgia. The boat was christened *The James Caird*, after the Scottish manufacturer who helped finance the expedition. In today's terms he gave over £1 million, more than twice the contribution of the British government.

Shackleton and five companions set out in the 20ft open boat, taking only four weeks' supplies, knowing that if they hadn't reached South Georgia within that time both boat and crew would be lost. They made landfall in fifteen days, only to be faced with a thirty-six hour hike over mountainous terrain to reach the whaling station at Stromness. Shackleton took just two companions on this last leg. In 1955, the British explorer, Duncan Carse, who successfully crossed the same overland route wrote, 'I do not know how they did it, except they had to – three men of the heroic age of Antarctic exploration with 50 feet of rope between them – and a carpenter's adze'.

The James Caird was retrieved and, when not away on display elsewhere, is now preserved at Dulwich College, Shackleton's old school in south London. She sits in the north cloisters on a bed of rocks imported from South Georgia.

Shackleton then immediately set about arranging the rescue of the rest of the party on the other side of South Georgia, those back on Elephant Island and also the men from their supply ship *Aurora*, the Ross Sea party, who had become stranded at Cape Evans in McMurdo Sound. Their ship had broken loose from its anchorage and driven out to sea.

However, Shackleton had such a reputation as a leader that 'His men – stranded, rescued, returned. They never doubted.'

'The Boss / inspired, inspiring' also had a poetical streak, as a Union-Castle Line shipmate remarked, 'spouting lines from Keats [and Browning], / 'lines by heart'. He enjoyed poetry and himself penned evocative phrases and the occasional poem, remarking, 'Teachers should be very careful not to spoil [their pupils'] taste for poetry for all time by making it a task and an imposition'.

'But a heart that failed' refers to his fatal heart attack on his last (1921) expedition. He died on 5 January 1922 while his ship, *Quest*, was moored in South Georgia. After an autopsy, his body was placed in a wooden coffin and taken first to the Whalers Church. Later it went by ship to Montevideo accompanied by one of his long-serving officers, a veteran of the *Endurance* expedition, bound for home. However, upon hearing of this intention Lady Shackleton requested that his remains be returned to Grytviken to be buried there, in the Polar Regions that meant so much to him. So it was that on 5 March 1922 about 100 men, mainly islanders, gathered for the funeral service back at the Whalers Church. The only woman on the island provided the flowers. Following the ceremony the coffin was carried by six Shetlanders to the cemetery for the interment.

The grave remained marked by a rough wooden cross for six years, until in 1928 the carved Scottish granite headstone was unveiled by the governor of the Falkland Islands. Around the grave a number of plaques have also appeared, including:

This tribute to The Boss is placed here by the crew of the ship bearing his name.
RRS *Shackleton* 1980/81

'Now written in stone, / A line to remember a life' refers to the quotation from Robert Browning on the gravestone, 'I hold that a man should strive in the uttermost for his life's set prize'.

The goal of Shackleton's repeated expeditions was to be the first man to reach the South Pole. This was his 'life's set prize'. When not on expeditions, Shackleton was restless. Various business ventures failed. He never succeeded in amassing personal wealth. He put most of his effort into fundraising for his expeditions. For the *Endurance* expedition of 1914 he raised the present-day equivalent of some £3 million, mainly from private donations. This greatly exceeded the British government funding. He died around £40,000 in debt (equivalent to over £1.5 million today). His widow and children would have faced a bleak future.

However, the nation was not about to let this happen. A memorial service was arranged at St Paul's Cathedral at which the king and other members of the royal family were represented. A biography, *The Life of Sir Ernest Shackleton*, was written by Hugh Robert Mill which raised money from royalties and further brought home his heroism to the general public. Additionally, a memorial fund was set up to undertake further fundraising to support his widow and children.

The final four lines of the poem are concerned with the many ways in which the name of Shackleton and the *Endurance* still live on. HMS *Endurance*, a modern Class 1 icebreaker built in Norway in 1990, deploys for seven months of the year to the Antarctic and South Atlantic. Her motto, in the spirit of Shackleton, is *'fortitudine vincimus'* ('by endurance we conquer'). The RRS *Shackleton*, a research ship also built in Norway in 1995, was acquired and so named by the British Antarctic Survey in August 1999. A Virgin Super Voyager train is named *Sir Ernest Shackleton*, and active in maritime reconnaissance and anti-submarine work in the 1950s and 1960s was the Avro Shackleton, used by the Royal Air Force.

One of the more unusual tributes was the naming of a crater on the moon as the Shackleton crater. It is, of course, near the moon's south pole. For philatelists, there is also the chance to collect postage stamps picturing Shackleton or the *Endurance*. At various times these have been issued, in particular by the Falkland Islands and the British Antarctic Territory. In 2014 the Post Office also issued the 'Ernest Shackleton's Antarctic Expedition Stamp Cover – BCSP32A' to celebrate the centenary of the *Endurance* expedition. This is particularly appropriate, as following Shackleton's second expedition, *Nimrod*, the New Zealand authorities had appointed him as Antarctic postmaster.

His legacy also 'lives in history' through the Shackleton Foundation (2007), in people-centred leadership courses and events in the UK, Ireland (his birthplace) and the USA – Shackleton being cited by the US Navy as a model leader. He has also been the subject of many books, and a Channel 4 Emmy award-winning TV serial, and several re-enactments of his expeditions have taken place. The 8th August 2014 also marked the start of the centenary of the *Endurance* Expedition. A full calendar of events (2014–17) can be found on www.Shackleton100.org.

The expedition is recognised as an unsurpassed epic feat of endurance and survival, the last major expedition of the heroic age of Antarctic exploration. Shackleton has provided an enduring model of leadership, as relevant to today's business executives and to those in authority in all walks of life, as it was among the ice floes and stormy seas of the Antarctic.

The James Caird Society, a charity registered in 1994, is still active in preserving Shackleton's memory. Although it was Captain Robert Falcon Scott who, at the time, was rated the greater hero, this had been reversed by the time a 2002 BBC poll was conducted to determine the '100 Greatest Britons'. Shackleton was ranked eleventh while Scott was in fifty-fourth place.

Finally, perhaps we all need to bear in mind Shackleton's advice, 'Difficulties are just things to overcome, after all'.

LIVING WITH ANGELS

Poet, painter, printmaker.
Romantic visionary,
'glorious luminary',
but genius or madman?

Born out of time, scant schooling.
Drawing in the abbey,
Michelangelo at his elbow.
Learning his craft, making his mark,
graven images.

Commissioned. A patron, a man of independent means
and good intentions.
'Away to sweet Felpham, for heaven is there',
away to England's green and pleasant land.

Troubled times, changing times,
intense emotions,
Revolution, reaction, revival,
art, literature, life, set free.

The idyll ends.
Out of that world, out of this world, into his.
Images in rhyme, images in the margins,
images in the mind,
art and poetry intertwined.
Mystical, mythical, songs of innocence,
songs of experience, Revelations.

Genesis ... recreated.
His cause ... no senseless wars, oppressive laws.

A tombstone for an unmarked grave,
a statue in the abbey.
Writers, poets, painters,
composers, singers, players,
the offspring of the inner man,
born out of time.
'Did he who made the Lamb make thee?'

24

WILLIAM BLAKE
POET AND ARTIST

William Blake was born in London on 28 November 1757, and died there on 12 August 1827. His parents kept a hosier's shop in Broad Street, central London; he was educated and learnt his trade in London and worked there for most of his life. He considered himself very much a Londoner. However, a defining moment in his life was not in London but in Sussex.

With his wife Catherine, at the age of 43, he came to stay for three years (1800–03) in a cottage in the village of Felpham, on the coast near Bognor Regis. This was at the invitation of a patron, a local poet and biographer, William Hayley, who wanted Blake to illustrate his own works. This was not a very interesting or creative job but Blake was grateful for Hayley's generosity. The Sussex countryside was also a welcome escape from the confines of London streets:

> Away to sweet Felpham, for heaven is there
> The ladder of Angels descends through the air.

Hayley was 'a man of independent means and good intentions'. The cottage was on his estate. Although well-meaning, his involvement was almost always counter to the wishes of those he helped, although stopping short of being a control freak. He was not in sympathy with Blake's visionary genius. Blake summed up their own relationship in the lines:

> Thy friendship oft has made my heart to ache:
> Do be my enemy for Friendship's sake.

At this point it is worth saying a few words about Catherine. She supported her 'difficult' husband in everything he did. Theirs was a lifelong, near forty-five-year partnership in work and in life. Blake taught her how to read, write, draw, engrave and colour his prints. Although the designs were always William's, some of the works held in national collections may also owe something to Catherine.

In Felpham he was feeling rather stifled in his work by the constraints placed upon him by Hayley. He needed a diversion. One of Hayley's biographical works was a life of Milton. At one point he was reputed to have sat naked in the garden reading *Paradise Lost* to Catherine ... after all, Milton's poem was about Adam and Eve. Hayley's book on Milton perhaps sowed the seed of an idea. Feeling the need to 'do his own thing', he made time to write a short preface to what was later to become *Milton: A Poem in Two Books*, an epic work that took him four years to complete. The preface concluded with a short lyrical poem that began,

'And did those feet in ancient time ...' and ended, 'In England's green and pleasant Land'. It was, of course, to become the hymn 'Jerusalem' which has become
another national anthem for many.

Later, on his return to London he referred to Felpham as the 'sweetest spot on
earth'. Sussex was the inspiration for his 'green and pleasant land' and he credited
'Jerusalem' to the result of 'three years' slumber on the banks of the Ocean'.

Towards the end of his three-year stay, though, 'the idyll ends'. These were
'troubled times, changing times'. Britain was under threat from the French
in the shape of Emperor Napoleon. In August 1803, rather unwisely William
Blake fell into a political argument with a soldier in the cottage garden. The soldier reported the incident to a higher authority. Blake was charged with
sedition and treason. It was his word against that of the soldier. The charges
were thrown out, but the spell was broken and William and Catherine returned
to London.

'Out of that world, out of this world, into his' is about more than the return
to London. William Blake literally 'lived in his own world'. The poem title 'Living
with Angels' is how Blake perceived his surroundings. Blake's inner life of
visions of angels, often all around him, and of monks and priests processing in
Westminster Abbey, were as real to him as flesh and blood people. According
to some accounts, Blake's first vision may have occurred at the age of 4 when
he saw God 'put his head to the window'. Another reported incident was a few
years later in Peckham Rye when he claimed to have seen 'a tree filled with
angels'. In *Favourite Hymns*, compiled by Marjorie Reeves and Jenyth Worsley,
the authors recount the theory that Blake may have suffered from 'eidetic
perception, which means that he experienced abstract ideas or metaphors as
actual people or angels who were with him in his own physical space'.

At the time, contemporaries just labelled him as mad or insane. Without this
condition, though, it is unlikely that we would now have 'Jerusalem'. This was, at
least in part, inspired by one of his childhood visions. The legend of Joseph of
Arimathea bringing Jesus as a boy to Glastonbury in Somerset was real to him.
He had seen 'those feet in ancient time walk upon England's mountains green'
and 'the Holy Lamb of God on England's pleasant pastures seen'.

Blake's parents were Dissenters, men and women who left the Church of
England and who opposed state involvement in religious faith. They protested
against what they considered oppressive laws and argued for a fair economy
and 'a heaven on this earth'. This was the background from which William Blake's
own philosophy sprang. Blake left school at the age of 10, his formal schooling
being largely confined to learning to read and write – 'scant schooling'. Apart
from this, his early education was down to his mother. At age 10 he attended
drawing classes, followed five years later by a seven-year apprenticeship with
an engraver. During this period, on one of his regular drawing assignments
in Westminster Abbey in 1774 – 'Drawing in the Abbey, Michelangelo at his
elbow' – the Westminster Abbey website entry on William Blake reports that
'he was an onlooker at the opening of the tomb of King Edward I and drew

pictures of the body in the coffin'. Shortly after completion of his apprentice-ship he entered the Royal Academy schools.

'Learning his craft, making his mark, graven images' refers to Blake's devel-opment as an engraver. In a departure from conventional engraving practice, for most of his well-known works Blake used his innovative technique of 'relief etching' or 'illuminated printing'. For his mass-market commercial work, though, he used the conventional intaglio engraving process. This was the 'bread and butter' of his meagre income for most of his life. It wasn't until later in his life that his more ambitious works began to sell, mainly to wealthy patrons.

As well as his own illuminated books, he illustrated works or painted water-colours inspired by the writings of such as Mary Wollstonecraft, John Gay, John Milton, John Bunyan, Dante Alighieri and William Shakespeare, as well as the books of the Bible.

The lines in Verse 5, 'Images in rhyme, images in the margins ... art and poetry intertwined', describe the appearance of his illuminated prints. Blake went back to the tradition of the illuminated manuscripts produced by the early Christian monks roughly between the eighth and fourteenth centuries. He greatly admired medieval and Gothic art. His own illuminated prints also combined handwritten text with images not only in the margins but snaking through the text. His subjects, though, were not confined solely to the biblical. His own poems were 'mystical, mythical', as were the images. The lines 'songs of inno-cence, songs of experience' are the titles of two of his collections. The former (1789) contains nineteen poems, including *Little Lamb, who made thee?*, the latter (1794) contains twenty-seven poems, including *The Tyger* ('Tyger Tyger, burn-ing bright'). The images were striking and the rhymes were memorable. Blake's poem *The Tyger* is one of the most reproduced poems ever written and was No. 18 in a poll of the Nation's Favourite Poems carried out in 1995. He called his poems 'songs' because that was how he meant them to be performed.

Both Blake's illustrations and his watercolours were also often disturb-ing. Their titles reflect this, *The Wood of the Self-Murderers: The Harpies and the Suicides*, *The Great Red Dragon and the Woman Clothed with Sun* (from Revelations 12: 1–5), and *The Lovers' Whirlwind* (illustration of hell in Canto V of Dante's *Inferno*) – not for those of a nervous disposition.

Blake is considered to be Pre-Romantic, as well as one of the key figures in the ensuing Romantic period. This was at its peak in the UK between about 1800 and 1850. The start of the Romantic Movement is often dated to the publica-tion in 1798 of the *Lyrical Ballads* of Wordsworth and Coleridge. Wordsworth was 28 and Coleridge 26. At the age of 41, Blake was much the elder member. Apart from these three, over time the other poets involved were Lord Byron, Shelley and Keats. At the outset, though, John Keats was still a toddler and so not writing that much.

The movement was partly a reaction to the Industrial Revolution, although William Blake was also influenced by the ideals and ambitions of the French and American Revolutions. The movement endorsed 'intense emotions', even horror and terror. The movement also extolled the beauty of nature and revived medievalism. It was a time of 'Revolution, reaction, revival, art, literature, life, set free'. J.M.W. Turner had taken landscape painting to the limits of Romanticism. Beethoven had produced 'monstrous and immeasurable' music. Wagner had written his Romantic period operas *Tännhauser* and *Lohengrin*. Right across the arts it was a time of high emotion and often the rejection of 'realism' and accepted techniques and values. Although William Blake was largely unrecognised during his lifetime, 'born out of time', he is now considered one of the figures of that age who has had perhaps the greatest influence on his successors.

Blake, from an early age, was a political as well as an artistic revolutionary. This aspect of his character is picked up by phrases in the poem, 'intense emotions, Revolution, reaction' and 'His cause ... no senseless wars, oppressive laws'. Blake was not a member of any regular political party, though. He was more of a go-it-alone anarchist than a 'joiner'. As a result of his childhood upbringing, the same could be said of his attitude to 'dogmatic' state religion, although in this case he did join a dissenting faith group, the Swedenborgian Society.

As hinted at in the line 'Genesis ... recreated', Blake was alone among his contemporaries in the degree to which he brought religion into his art and poetry. He had his own twist on the Bible, however. In his work he favoured the historical and mythical, illustrating specific characters, events or phrases. In the case of Dante, Milton, Shakespeare and the Greek myths, this was fine. In the case of the Old Testament of the Bible, however, he had a problem. The problem was his rejection of the accepted theology.

As J. Bronowski points out in his *Introduction to William Blake*, 'Blake's form of Christianity was heretical, for it identified Christ the Son with all spiritual goodness and made God the Father a symbol of terror and tyranny'. So, not content only to use existing myths and characters, Blake created his own. This is reflected in the words that Blake put into the mouth of Los in *Jerusalem, The Emanation of the Giant Albion* (1804–20), 'I must create a system or be enslaved by another man's; I will not reason and compare: my business is to create'. In Blake's recreation of Old Testament theology, Los is the hero, a Christlike figure, as in the New Testament, in contrast to the jealous and fearful God of the Old Testament, whom Blake calls Urizen. It gets more complicated.

One of Blake's most famous images is *The Ancient of Days*. This is a phrase denoting God, familiar to Christians in the hymn 'Immortal, invisible. God only Wise'. The image combines a vision from the Book of Daniel (7: 9, 22) with an event in the Book of Proverbs (8: 27). It shows a bearded old man with 'the hair of his head like pure wool: his throne was like the fiery flame ... setting a compass upon the face of the depth'. All well and good, to Blake, however, his *Ancient of Days* depicted his character Urizen from his *Book of Urizen*, his alternative Book of Genesis.

Worse was to come. Blake used a similar image in an illustration entitled *Newton*, who is seated on a rock by a dark sea, oblivious of what may be going on around him, absorbed in measuring on the ground with a (smaller) pair of compasses. Blake strongly criticised Isaac Newton for putting science and reason above the poetic or prophetic. He wrote, 'save us from Newton's blindness'. To ram home his point Blake declared, 'Art is the tree of life. Science is the tree of death.' In two images he had risked offending both Christians and scientists, although many may not have grasped his hidden messages.

Peter Ackroyd, in his biography *Blake*, describes events on the day of Blake's death. Blake worked feverishly right up to a few hours before the end, determined to try and finish his illustrations to Dante's *Inferno*. Eventually he admitted defeat. His last drawing was of his wife, in tears by his bedside, 'for you have ever been an angel to me'. It was just a few days short of their forty-fifth wedding anniversary. He then laid down his pencil and 'raised his voice to the Lord', singing hymns and verses. As George Richmond wrote in a letter to fellow artist Samuel Palmer, 'singing of the things he saw in Heaven'.

William Blake died in poverty in 1827 at the age of 69. He is buried in the same area as Daniel Defoe and John Bunyan in the Dissenters' Graveyard in London's Bunhill Fields Cemetery. His was an unmarked grave. Four years later Catherine joined him. There is now a tombstone on the approximate site. They had no children, but his genes lived on in 'Writers, poets, painters, composers, singers, players, the offspring of the inner man'.

The nineteenth-century scholar William Rossetti characterised him as a 'glorious luminary'. A contemporary art critic proclaimed him 'far and away the greatest artist Britain has ever produced'. In 2002, Blake was placed at No. 38 in the BBC's poll of the 100 Greatest Britons.

A roll-call of those upon whom his light has shone would include:

1   The poets and writers W.B. Yeats, C.S. Lewis, J.G. Ballard, the Beat Poets of the 1950s (especially Allen Ginsberg, who also set several Blake poems to music), Philip Pullman (*His Dark Materials*), Tracy Chevalier (*Burning Bright*) and Thomas Harris (*Silence of the Lambs*).
2   Songwriters and popular musicians, including Bob Dylan and Jim Morrison (The Doors).
3   The Pre-Raphaelite artists (particularly Dante Gabriel Rossetti), Paul Nash, Dora Carrington and Graham Sutherland.
4   Composers, who set his words to music: Benjamin Britten, Ralph Vaughan Williams, John Tavener and Sir Charles Parry ('Jerusalem', of course, became the special anthem of the WI and is also a highlight at the Last Night of the Proms at the Royal Albert Hall. Sir Hubert Parry was the composer who discovered the words in the First World War and set them to music in 1916).

Blake's books incorporating 'illuminated printing' were the forerunners of today's graphic novels, and his images that of fantasy art. TV and filmmakers have also used his poems or images. The film title *Chariots of Fire* was inspired by a phrase from 'Jerusalem'.

As well as William and Catherine's tombstone and the bust in Poet's Corner in Westminster Abbey, there are memorial plaques at connected sites, including one on the cottage at Felpham. In September 2015, following a successful appeal by the Blake Society, the purchase of Blake's Cottage was completed and is now held in trust for the nation in perpetuity.

Blake's tomb is still, to some, a pilgrimage site. The last line of the poem, 'Did he who made the Lamb make thee?' taken from *The Tyger*, took on a new significance when, as Roger Tagholm reported in *Walking Literary London*, on a cold, windy day in March 1999 the words were found spelt out in different coloured strips of Plasticine in front of William Blake's tombstone.

EN AVANT

Schooled at his Chelsea home,
drawing, observing. Euclid.
Father, the engineer passing on
his language, his skills.

Schooled on the Sussex coast,
surveying, a wager won. Virgil.
Schooled in his father's land,
lycée, université. Breguet.

Returned. The engineer –
Steamships, bridges, tracks,
largest, longest, fastest.
Bold plans, but right – Firsts,
the wonders of his world.

Under rivers, over rivers,
boring through hills, nothing deterred.
Timber, brick and iron.
A little man but
a giant shadow.

But not all steamships, bridges, tracks.
Scutari, Swindon,
unlikely midwives.
Scutari, a prayer answered,
an engineer's solution,
'those magnificent huts' – a model.

Swindon, railway village, hospital,
clinics, duty of care – a model.
One hundred years, one birth,
available to all,
free at the point of use.

And the engineer? A death too soon but a lasting legacy,
one of our greatest.
En Avant.

25

ISAMBARD KINGDOM BRUNEL
ENGINEER

The poem title *'En Avant'* ('Forward') was Brunel's personal motto, inscribed on his signet ring. Brunel liked to translate his French motto as 'get going'. His father, Sir Marc Isambard Brunel, was a French civil engineer, a refugee from the French Revolution, who married an English girl, Sophia Kingdom. They had first met in France, where the teenaged Sophia had been sent to learn the language, but they soon had to go separate ways. They met up again in England in 1799 and were married. By then Marc was 30 and Sophia about five years younger. They settled in Portsmouth, near Marc's work, and already had two daughters by the time their only son, Isambard Kingdom Brunel, was born on 9 April 1806. Two years later the family moved to the 'village' of Chelsea on the River Thames.

People sometimes remark on Brunel's unusual first names. As can now be seen, 'Kingdom' came from his mother's surname before marriage. 'Isambard', also one of his father's first names, has a long history. It is a Norman name of Germanic origin. For a family of engineers of the eighteenth and nineteenth centuries it was particularly appropriate. It can be interpreted variously as 'iron-bright', 'glittering iron', 'iron giant' or 'man of iron'.

Brunel's early schooling was in this family home in Chelsea. From the age of 4 his father taught him drawing and observational techniques before moving on to Euclidian geometry and the basic principles of engineering. He was, of course, also bilingual, a fluent French speaker. .

At some point between the ages of 8 and 14 (accounts vary) he attended Dr Morrell's Academy, a boarding school in Hove in a terrace south-east of Hove Street, facing the seafront. It was demolished in the 1930s when Kingsway was widened. He liked the Classics. In a letter home to his mother in 1820 he writes, 'I like Horace very much, but not as much as Virgil'. In his spare time he made model boats and also drew up a 'pretty exact plan' of Hove as it then was. To improve on its accuracy he even asked to borrow his father's 'long eighty foot tape ... I will take care of it'.

One aspect of the observational techniques his father had taught him was to identify any faults in the structure of a building. This proved to be profitable. In the comprehensive biography, *The Life of Isambard Kingdom Brunel, Civil Engineer*, his son, also Isambard, tells the story. One evening Brunel had noticed the bad workmanship on some houses being built opposite the school and with the stormy weather worsening during the night, predicted that their walls would have blown down by the morning! The other boys readily accepted his bet. As was to be the case for most of his life, he was right, and claimed the wagers next morning.

Brunel left Dr Morrell's in 1820 at the age of 14 to continue his education in France, his father's wish. His main schooling was at the Collège Henri Quatre in Paris. Following this, his father's wish was for him to attend the famous university-level engineering school, École Polytechnique, but being of foreign birth he was ineligible. Brunel was therefore apprenticed to one of the most famous master clockmakers and horologists of all time, Abraham-Louis Breguet, whom he greatly impressed. The Breguet Company is now the luxury watch division of the Swiss Swatch Group.

Upon the completion of his apprenticeship, Brunel returned to London and worked as an assistant to his father on the construction of the Thames Tunnel. This was the first tunnel under a river anywhere in the world. It was deemed 'The Eighth Wonder of the World' and was a major tourist attraction. Started in 1825, it opened for pedestrians in 1843 but not for trains until 1869. During construction there had been severe flooding and several deaths. In one of these floods Isambard Kingdom Brunel himself was nearly killed, having to be dragged unconscious from the floodwater. He was off work for six months and did not return to the project.

He then secured a position as chief engineer of the Great Western Railway (GWR). It was Brunel's vision that passengers would be able to buy one ticket at Paddington for travel from London to New York. This would require building a railway from London, via Bristol, requiring some 100 bridges, viaducts and tunnels, to a projected steamship terminal in Neyland, west Wales. It would also require the design and construction of commercially viable transatlantic steamships. This was of course regarded as an impossible pipe (or cigar) dream.

His first radical decision was to abandon George Stephenson's original standard-gauge track width (4ft 8¼in) in favour of his new broad gauge (7ft ¼in). This would enable higher speeds, a smoother ride and greater passenger and freight capacity. This was a battle that he lost, though, and following the Regulating the Gauge of Railways Act 1846, the GWR network was forced to change to standard gauge.

And then there were his bridges. Chapter 23 of Magna Carta states, 'No town or person shall be forced to build bridges over rivers except those with an ancient obligation to do so', but Brunel revelled in the challenge. His two most famous bridges are probably the beautiful Clifton Suspension Bridge (started in 1831 but not completed until 1864) at Bristol, and the bowstring-girder Royal Albert Bridge (opened in 1859, the year of Brunel's death) across the River Tamar at Saltash, near Plymouth.

The span of the Clifton Suspension Bridge, symbol of the City of Bristol, was the longest of his time. The bridge was based on the 24-year-old Brunel's original designs, but with later significant changes by two other engineers (William Henry Barlow and Sir John Hawshaw). The feature that even Brunel's father did not think possible, a single span without a centre support, was, however, realised. Right again! Brunel referred to his Clifton Suspension Bridge proudly as, 'My darling ... my first child'.

Throughout his life Brunel was not afraid to attempt the impossible. 'The man with the greatest originality of thought and power of execution, bold in his plans but right ... great things are not done by those who sit down and count the cost of every thought and act' (taken from Brunel's epitaph and written by Sir Daniel Gooch, chairman of the GWR).

As a result of his education and training in mathematics and engineering Brunel was not only sound in his theory but took a very practical approach to implementation. He certainly did not just 'sit down' and draw up designs on paper. He first surveyed the terrain personally and exhaustively, just as with his boyhood intention to make an exact plan of Hove while he was at Dr Morrell's Academy. In the case of the banks of the River Avon, it was also exhausting for his helper. He roped in his Bristol solicitor to row him down the river to survey the riverbanks, in order to determine the best design for the bridge and its exact location. His solicitor's opinion of being 'volunteered' is not recorded.

On a subsequent occasion, when building started there was the problem of transporting materials across. His biographer records how Brunel came up with the solution. A 1,000ft iron bar was suspended between the two ends with a man-sized basket to be pulled back and forth by ropes. Brunel was, of course, the first person to test it. Inevitably the rope became snagged and he was left dangling in mid-air some 200ft above river level. Brunel was not at all worried. He just climbed out of the basket, freed the rope and continued – no bother. The episode brought huge publicity – shades of the memorable press photos of former London Mayor Boris Johnson similarly stuck on his zip wire!

As mentioned in Verse 4, however, Brunel did not only build in wrought iron (cheap steel was not available until several decades after his death). He also built in brick. The Maidenhead Railway Bridge, at the time the flattest, widest arch bridge in the world, is still carrying trains to the west. He built to last – today's trains are about ten times heavier than in his time. He also made extensive use of timber, particularly for viaducts.

Another impossible project was Box Tunnel, through Box Hill in Wiltshire. It was, naturally, the longest railway tunnel in the world at the time. As the poem says, 'Bold plans, but right – Firsts, the wonders of his world'.

And so we reach the west coast. Now what of the steamships, the extension of the GWR across the Atlantic to New York? Before the GWR had even opened, the Great Western Steamship Company was formed. The company entrusted Brunel with designing its first ship, SS *Great Western*. Using mathematics based on experimental evidence, Brunel convinced his doubters that a large ship would take proportionately less fuel than a smaller ship. To carry enough fuel to cross the Atlantic required a very large ship. The SS *Great Western* (1838) again set new records – the longest ship in the world, the first ship to hold the Blue Riband, with an average crossing time of just under thirteen days, and the first to be commercially successful. Brunel was asked to design a sister ship.

Always an innovator, this time he eschewed a mainly wooden construction with paddle wheels and supplementary masts for sails, for an iron-hulled, propeller-driven ship. This was the SS *Great Britain* (1843), the first 'modern' ship, now fully preserved and open to the public in Bristol.

Brunel's final ship, SS *Great Eastern* (maiden voyage 1860), was perhaps a step too far. Even larger than her predecessors, she was designed to carry over 4,000 passengers in luxury, non-stop from London to Sydney. She remained the largest ship ever built until the start of the twentieth century. Technologically she was a success, years ahead of her time, however, commercially she was a disaster. Although never viable for her intended purpose, she notched up another first as an oceanic cable-laying ship – laying the first lasting transatlantic telegraph cable. A famous photo shows Brunel dwarfed by the launching chains of the *Great Eastern*. The only surviving piece of the ship is the flagpole, which stands at the entrance to Anfield (Liverpool Football Club's ground).

Brunel was not all about 'steamships, bridges, tracks', however. Following a plea from Florence Nightingale, the government commissioned him to design and have built a temporary hospital of prefabricated huts incorporating Florence Nightingale's hygiene requirements. When finished, this was shipped to the Crimea. Renkioi Hospital, as it was known, was erected near Scutari Hospital, Nightingale's base, which it replaced. It cut the death toll to around one-tenth of its predecessor. Nightingale referred to it as 'those magnificent huts'.

Swindon's nineteenth-century 'railway village', built for Brunel's GWR workers, incorporated a 'hospital, clinics [and] duty of care'. Membership of its Medical Fund Society, founded in 1841 by Sir Daniel Gooch, first locomotive superintendent of the GWR at Swindon (and later GWR chairman), was a condition of employment for the railway workers. Another world first.

Both Renkioi Hospital and the Swindon 'Local Health Service' were models for the establishment of the National Health Service (NHS) by Aneurin Bevan 100 years later. The founding principle of the NHS was 'available to all, free at the point of use'.

Isambard Kingdom Brunel died at the age of 53, ten years after the death of his father. Both men died from strokes. Brunel was often seen in photographs with a large cigar in hand or mouth, a heavy smoker. 'A little man but a giant shadow' – he was just over 5ft tall, hence the distinctive 8in high stove-pipe hat, 'I catch myself trying to look big on my little pony'. His 'giant shadow', his legacy, is commemorated by statues, street names, schools, pubs, a shopping centre, a university (Brunel), museums, named locomotives, and films and documentaries. Recently, and most memorably, he was portrayed by Kenneth Branagh at the 2012 Summer Olympics Opening Ceremony in a segment showing the Industrial Revolution. The ceremony also highlighted the NHS.

Returning to the Hove connection, in being nominated one of the 100 Greatest Britons in a TV poll of 2002, Brunel was second only to another great Briton who attended school in the town when he was a small boy – Sir Winston Churchill.

To end with, some quotes. Brunel was always single-mindedly focussed on the task in hand and today we might call him a control freak, a fault that he admitted. Despite his happy marriage he wrote in his diary, '... my profession is after all my only fit wife'. Finally, this persisting image of the committed engineer is also neatly illustrated by a conversation reported by Herbert Hoover, the 31st President of the United States from 1929 to 1933. By training at Stanford University, Hoover was a mining engineer. As president, he spearheaded the construction of the St Lawrence Seaway and the Hoover Dam. On making the acquaintance of a lady on a steamship:

'Tell me, Mr Hoover, what are your interests?'
'Madam, I am an Engineer'
'Really? I took you for a gentleman.'

It was, though, apparently meant as a compliment!

MASTER OF THE MOON

Fearless eccentric, no amateur, no dinosaur
but equally irreplaceable,
the last of a generation.
Knight of the night sky,
his footprint on the moon.

Magic. Weaving his spell,
planting seeds in young minds,
a mission to inspire.
Apollo, Voyager, Pioneer.
Heroes met and heroes made, fact and fiction.

Researcher, observer, composer, performer –
twin loves. His mother's gift,
his was no monocular vision.

A household name, father figure, cat protector,
his master's lap the centre of Ptolemy's universe.
Parties in the garden, nights to remember,
a generous host, Farthings' rules.
Yet a household denied his first lost love,
substance and shadows.

Every minute filled, but forever in his thoughts
those unlived lives, until,
his daily paper uncollected, obituaries unread,
he's there, his distance run.

For the party-goers, nectar and soda
at the pearly gates.
And that lost love, those unlived lives?
'Our bodies die, we do not die,
not pointless, I'm sure she's there'.

26

SIR PATRICK MOORE

AMATEUR ASTRONOMER AND MUSICIAN

Sir Patrick Alfred Caldwell-Moore CBE, FRS, FRAS (4 March 1923–9 December 2012) was a man of many talents – 'his was no monocular vision' (his monocle, worn due to his right eye being weaker than his left, was one of his distinguishing features). He was an inspiring interpreter of modern astronomy, instantly recognisable, appealingly eccentric and widely respected. He was the presenter of the world's longest running television series with the same original presenter (721 editions), the BBC's *The Sky at Night*. The series was launched in the same year as Sputnik 1 (1957), and his last appearance was just a week before his death in 2012.

In 1968 he moved into 'Farthings' in Selsey, West Sussex, a partly thatched house complete with resident bats in the roof. Parts of the house date back to the seventeenth century. One of his first tasks was to supervise the building of an observatory (later joined by another three) in his garden. His companions were his mother, Gertrude, until her death aged 84 in 1981, a succession of much-loved cats, and countless visitors and house guests, always welcome. He was 'a generous host', 'Farthings' rules' (Verse 4) refer to his insistence that guests just help themselves to drinks at all times without asking.

In the field of astronomy he was a widely respected researcher ('no amateur'), writer (over seventy books), radio commentator, TV presenter and contributor, guest speaker and president of the British Astronomical Association. 'Apollo, Voyager, Pioneer' are, of course, the names by which some of the American (NASA) space programmes were known, and upon which Moore commentated for BBC television. His lunar mapping was of great value to the moon missions and he acted as a consultant with both American and Soviet space programmes.

Also in the opening line of the poem, 'no dinosaur' rebuts ill-judged remarks that he was 'old-fashioned', had become 'a bit of a dinosaur'. He still typed his books and answered letters, at ninety words per minute, in the computer age, on his faithful 1908 Woodstock typewriter. Of course, in his terms ninety words per minute was slow. Sir Patrick's breakneck speech was commented upon by BBC science correspondent Pallab Ghosh, 'on occasions he would talk at 300 words a minute'. Viewers and listeners couldn't help but be swept up in his enthusiasm.

Sir Patrick also abhorred metrification; he was a patron of the British Weights and Measures Association. When in 1999 the Mars Orbiter spacecraft completely missed the planet due to NASA mistakenly calculating in kilometres rather than miles (a £78 million error), he felt justified – 'Just goes to show the dangers of the metric system'. His response to the 'dinosaur' criticism was typically pointed,

'I may be accused of being a dinosaur, but I would remind you that dinosaurs ruled the earth for a very long time'.

'Heroes met' refers to his wide-ranging contacts. He was perhaps the only person to have met the first man to fly (Orville Wright), the first in space (Yuri Gagarin) and the first on the moon (Neil Armstrong). Armstrong's fellow Apollo 11 moonwalker, Buzz Aldrin, was also later (2002) to present Moore with his special BAFTA award for services to television. This echoed the citation for his 2001 knighthood for 'Services to the popularisation of science and to broadcasting'. Another memorable encounter is

revealed by Moore's assertion, 'I'm only a four-dimensional creature. Haven't got a clue how to visualise infinity. Even Einstein hadn't. I know because I asked him.'

'Heroes made, fact and fiction' refers both to the fictional heroes he created in his science fiction novels for children and to those future leading lights in the field who were mesmerised by his 'magic' from an early age. He devoted a lot of time to 'Weaving his spell, / planting seeds in young minds, / a mission to inspire'. Brian Warner, emeritus professor of astronomy at the University of Cape Town, summed this up:

> There are many individuals in successive generations of professional astronomers who owe a great deal to the books and personal support of Patrick Moore. He introduced children of all ages to astronomy, and some of them became prominent professionals in astrophysics and planetary sciences.

His other television persona was as the *GamesMaster*, 1992–98 (126 episodes). He also appeared in a bewildering variety of radio and television programmes, from *Panorama* through *Morecombe & Wise*, *Children in Need*, *MasterChef* and as a panellist on a number of quiz programmes, to a cameo appearance on *Doctor Who* and a minor part in the fourth radio series of *The Hitchhiker's Guide to the Galaxy*. Back in Sussex, he was a keen amateur actor, appearing in local plays.

In addition to his science fiction novels for children he also wrote humorous works as R.T. Fishall. Sir Patrick's sense of humour and (un-PC) wit was well known. On one of his USA trips, when visiting Utah, he was welcomed by a local with the words, 'Welcome to the Mormon state. We are quite different from the rest of America. You will find no swearing or drinking or wild women here.'

Moore replied, 'It's hardly worth coming, is it?'

The poem title '*Master of the Moon*' is also the title of his first science fiction book for children, published in 1952. It was what he labelled 'my first boys' novel'. Moore's particular field of interest was moon observation, hence the poem title and the line 'his footprint on the Moon'. Of course his was a 'virtual' footprint, the real physical footprints were those of the Apollo 11 astronauts, Neil Armstrong and Buzz Aldrin.

'Composer, performer' refers to the fact that Moore was also an accomplished and knowledgeable musician. For the 1957 launch of *The Sky at Night*, an appropriate theme tune had to be chosen. He rejected the original proposal, 'You are my Lucky Star', as 'fluff' in favour of the first movement of Jean Sibelius's 'Pélleas et Mélisande: At the Castle Gate'. It became the permanent opener to the programme. He composed pieces for brass bands and piano and more than one opera. As a performer, his instruments were the xylophone, glockenspiel and piano. His sometime duettists included Evelyn Glennie, the profoundly deaf percussionist (also a xylophone player) and, as a pianist, surprisingly, Albert Einstein (violin). The latter event, on the occasion of their meeting in New York, was *not* recorded!

Although not really into modern rock songs, he enjoyed a close friendship with (Dr) Brian May, Queen guitarist and astrophysicist, who had rushed out to buy all Sir Patrick's books after his first viewing of *The Sky at Night* at about the age of 10. Later May was to become an occasional guest on the programme and, after Sir Patrick's death, one of the executors of his will. The 'twin loves' of music and astronomy, in Moore's case, 'His mother's gift', were also shared by Chris Lintott, fellow *Sky at Night* presenter and opera composer – three astronomers, three musicians.

Despite being 'A household name' he unsparingly gave his time to others. He 'adopted' the four sons of friends who had died relatively young, and indeed was a kind of father figure or caring uncle to many of the youngsters to whom he had passed on his own love of astronomy. He was also known for his charitable works. He helped raise money for victims of the 2005 Indian Ocean tsunami together with his good friend, science fiction writer and scientist, Arthur C. Clarke. Always the showman for a good cause, in 1982 he had also played xylophone with the BBC *Children in Need* band.

'Cat protector' refers to his love of cats and support of the Cats Protection charity. Bonnie, a stray black and white kitten, appeared in his garden one day asking to be adopted, 'There was no arguing with that. A catless house is a soulless house'. Upon Bonnie's death nearly twenty years later, Ptolemy took her place. Moore chose the name. The phrase 'the centre of Ptolemy's universe' merits further explanation.

Claudius Ptolemy (*c.* AD 90–*c.* AD 168) was a Greco-Egyptian mathematician and astronomer. Ptolemy expounded his geocentric (Earth centred) theory of the universe. This 'Ptolemaic Model' became the accepted model of the universe for some 1,400 years. It was gradually superseded, against strong theological opposition, by our true heliocentric (Sun centred) model by Copernicus, Galileo and Kepler. But the centre of his feline namesake's universe was surely Sir Patrick.

Despite his companion cats, his many visitors, the 'parties in the garden', the 'nights to remember', there was always someone missing – 'substance and shadows'. His fiancée, Lorna, a nurse, was killed at the age of 20 in a German air raid on London in 1943. The ambulance that she was driving was struck by a bomb. It was three years after they first met, 'That was it for me. There couldn't be anybody else.'

The penultimate verse is concerned with Sir Patrick's final days. The first and last phrases – 'Every minute filled … his distance run' – is taken from the final verse of what was found to be the Nation's Favourite Poem in a BBC poll taken in 1995, *If* by Rudyard Kipling:

> If you can fill the unforgiving minute
> With sixty seconds' worth of distance run,
> Yours is the Earth and everything that's in it,
> And – which is more – you'll be a Man, my son!

The lines, 'but forever in his thoughts / those unlived lives', of course refer back to Lorna. In an interview with the *Daily Mail* he revealed that rarely half an hour went by without his thinking of her. The other enclosed lines – 'until, / his daily paper uncollected, obituaries unread, / he's there' – remind us of his humour, his tendency to poke fun at himself, and his enjoyment of the good-natured ribbing he sometimes invited. The quote that he picked up on was originally that of Mark Twain, 'I get my copy of the daily paper, look at the obituaries page, and if I'm not there, I carry on as usual'. In editions after 12.25 on the afternoon of 9 December 2012, he *was* there. He died peacefully at his home in the company of close friends and carers, and of course his cat, Ptolemy.

But that was not the end. He thought that funerals were a waste of time and so he left money in his will to have a party, with musical accompaniment from one of his own compositions. It was of course to be a 'Farthings' Rules' occasion, to be extended in due course to the 'pearly gates' where he would welcome all with 'nectar and soda'.

The last three lines document his belief in an afterlife, in a chance to be reunited with Lorna, 'I don't believe partings are for ever. If we die when our bodies do, then everything would be pointless. And the universe is not pointless. The next stage? Oh, I'm sure she's there.'

In the meantime, for us earthbound mortals, his close friend and one of his executors, Brian May, explained in a post on his 'soapbox' (9 October 2015) the plans to establish a lasting legacy to Sir Patrick Moore. These include a permanent display and research facility at the Science Museum, the establishment of the Patrick Moore Heritage Trust, donations of some special items and funding to a 'thriving, teaching Chichester Planetarium', provisions relating to his music, his cricket and his support of the Herschel Museum in Bath. There are also, of course, the many archived appearances on TV and radio shows. As Brian May points out in his own tribute, though, 'Most of all, we all know that his greatest legacy is the current generation of top British astronomers, amateur and professional, who credit Patrick as their original inspiration to do what they do now'.

EXPLORER'S GUIDE

If this book has whetted your appetite for exploring Sussex places and people, you are invited to follow these waymarkers. The general pointers are followed by recommended specific sources to follow up for each chapter, including some excellent audio/video clips.

GENERAL

PRINT

Arscott, David, *The Little Book of Sussex* (Stroud: The History Press, 2011).

ArtFund, *The Art Guide* (Melksham: NACF, 2015. Provided as part of Art Fund membership, whose membership cards enable free or reduced price admission to over 270 charging museums, galleries, castles and historic houses).

Brandon, Peter, *The Discovery of Sussex* (Andover: Phillimore, 2010).

Brickell, Christopher (ed.), *The RHS New Encyclopaedia of Plants and Flowers* (London: Dorling Kindersley, 1999).

Jenkins, Simon, *England's Thousand Best Houses* (London: Allen Lane, 2003).

Jones, Griff Rhys (foreword), *The Nation's Favourite Poems* (London: BBC, 1996).

McGough, Roger (foreword), *Poetry Please* (London: Faber and Faber, 2013).

National Trust, *The National Trust Handbook* (provided as part of National Trust membership, whose membership cards enable free access to over 500 properties and sites). There are similar membership schemes for English Heritage and the Sussex Archaeological Trust.

Sampson, Ana, *I Wandered Lonely as a Cloud ... and Other Poems you Half-remember from School* (London: Michael O'Mara Books Ltd, 2013).

INTERNET SOURCES

For those readers unfamiliar with internet sources (websites), the following sections include brief explanations:

http://en.wikipedia.org/wiki – Wikipedia is a free internet encyclopaedia, supported and hosted by the non-profit Wikimedia Foundation. It is written and edited collaboratively by the people who use it. It is the internet's largest and most popular general reference work. It is a good starting point, but although the level of accuracy is claimed to approach that of *Encyclopaedia Britannica*, it can be advisable to cross-check with other sources.

www.gutenberg.org – Project Gutenberg was the first provider of free electronic books (eBooks). It is non-profit, financed by donations, and powered totally by volunteers. There are now nearly 50,000 free eBooks on Gutenberg. All books are free to read online. It is particularly useful for looking up 'classics' e.g. Chaucer's *Canterbury Tales*, or Lewis Carroll's *Alice Through the Looking Glass*.

www.bbc.co.uk/yourpaintings – The entire UK national collection of over 200,000 oil paintings, stories behind the paintings and where to see them.

www.nationaltrust.org.uk – Contains extensive information on all National Trust sites and properties, including the collections of art and artefacts.

www.sussexpast.co.uk – The Sussex Archaeological Society website.

www.sussexlife.co.uk – *Sussex Life* magazine website.

http://history.buses.co.uk – The website of the Brighton & Hove Bus and Coach Company, on which the company provides brief biographies of all the people with a Sussex connection whose names appear on their buses. Click on 'Fleet History', then 'Current Fleet', then the name of the person.

The internet search engine used by the author was Google. As well as specific name, place and event searches, generalised search phrases to use include:
'Quotes by (or about) …'
'Images of …'
'Videos (or video clips) of (or about) …'
'Poems by (or about) …'

AUDIO/VIDEO CLIPS

www.youtube.com – video sharing website. Unregistered users can watch any videos. Registered users can also upload videos to the site. The vast majority of videos on YouTube are free to view and supported by advertising (a short advertisement is usually shown before the video starts).
www.bbc.co.uk/news – The BBC provides a large amount of their own material free to view.
https://vimeo.com – video sharing website. There is a free to join, free to view version called Vimeo Basic. For those wishing to upload videos to the site there are also two chargeable versions.

TOURIST INFORMATION CENTRES (TIC) AND PUBLIC LIBRARIES

TICs provide extensive ranges of free publicity leaflets and guides together with personal advice. Leaflets will also be found in public libraries and National Trust, English Heritage and Sussex Archaeological Trust properties. Public libraries in Sussex are well stocked with local history resources both for reference and loan.

ORDNANCE SURVEY MAPS

The relevant Sussex maps are Explorer Maps 120–124, 133–136 and Landranger Maps 197–199. The National Trust also produces a free map showing their properties, available to all.

CHAPTER SPECIFIC SOURCES

Note about websites: When you enter a specific web address (URL) it may sometimes come up with a 'not found' message. Assuming that you have typed in the URL accurately, this is because items are occasionally withdrawn or relocated. In this case, just carry out a more generalised search. For this purpose, and to explore further, at the end of each chapter's list of sources there is a section called 'Relevant websites found by searches for ...'. You can also cast a wider net, picking up the latest entries by using phrases such as 'Videos about ...', 'Images of ...', 'Quotes by or about ...' Happy hunting!

1 BATEMAN'S

PRINT

Kipling, Rudyard, *If* and *The Glory of the Garden in Jones, The Nation's Favourite Poems*. Kipling, Rudyard, *The Jungle Book* (Chapter 1 – 'Mowgli's Brothers').

AUDIO/VIDEO

A website search for 'The bare necessities song' provides links to several audio/video clips.
The most popular film adaptation of *The Jungle Book* is still that produced by Walt Disney Animation Studios in 1967, although a new live action/CGI version is due for release in 2016.
www.sussexexpress.co.uk/news/videos/video-kipling-s-great-nephew-launches-replica-of-the-poet-s-paddle-boat-at-bateman-s-1-3810003 (52 seconds).

WEBSITES

www.kiplingsociety.co.uk (current and historical material from the Kipling Society).

www.nationaltrust.org.uk/batemans (photographs and news items are changed to reflect the season).
www.nobelprize.org/nobel_prizes/literature/laureates/1907 (includes the text of the complete award ceremony speech and links to further information including a rare short video clip of a speech by Kipling to the Canadian Authors' Association).

Relevant websites found by searches for 'Rudyard Kipling', 'Bateman's', 'Nobel Prize for Literature', 'boating pond at Batemans'.

2   BEACHY HEAD, BIRLING GAP AND THE SEVEN SISTERS.

PRINT

Trend, Nick, '36 hours in ... the South Downs', *Daily Telegraph*, 29 May 2013.

AUDIO/VIDEO

www.bbc.co.uk/news/uk-england-sussex-26442187 (24 seconds: *Daily Telegraph* photographer Eddie Mitchell captured the moment that part of the Birling Gap cliff face collapsed – Tuesday, 4 March 2014).
www.youtube.com/watch?v=KVMq97i9juo (3 minutes 8 seconds: BBC *News 24*, 'Belle Tout Lighthouse Being Moved Inland', 17 March 1999).
www.youtube.com/watch?v=Hqtaoz4QFX8 (3 minutes 09 seconds: Vera Lynn sings 'The White Cliffs of Dover' – some of the images are of Beachy Head and the Seven Sisters).

WEBSITES

www.beachyhead.org.uk/education/history (includes the 'Parson Darby's Hole' account).
www.nationaltrust.org.uk/birling-gap-and-the-seven-sisters (includes archaeology project).

Relevant websites found by searches for 'Seven Sisters, Sussex', 'Birling Gap', 'Parson Darby's Hole', 'Belle Tout Lighthouse', 'Beachy Head Lighthouse', *The Lighthouse Keeper's Lunch*, '*Seascape*, poem by W.H. Auden', '*Seven Brides for Seven Brothers*', 'There'll be Blue Birds over the White Cliffs of Dover', 'The South Downs Way'.

3   ALFRISTON CLERGY HOUSE

PRINT

Jenkins, Simon, *England's Thousand Best Houses* (p.746).

AUDIO/VIDEO

https://vimeo.com/26006815 (6 minutes 51 seconds: 'Octavia Hill' – a short video biography from the National Trust, including the purchase of Alfriston Clergy House by the trust).

WEBSITES

www.nationaltrust.org.uk/alfriston-clergy-house.

Relevant websites found by searches for 'Alfriston Clergy House', 'Octavia Hill', 'Sir Robert Hunter', 'Canon Hardwicke Rawnsley', 'St Andrew's Church, Alfriston', 'Judas Tree', 'Old London Waterloo Bridge', 'Octavia Hill rose'.

4   CHARLESTON & MONK'S HOUSE

PRINT

'Angela Garnett: Obituary', *The Telegraph*, 7 May 2012.
Banks, Joanne Trautmann (ed.), *Vintage Woolf: Selected Letters*.
Bell, Anne Olivier (ed.), *The Diary of Virginia Woolf*, Volumes 1–5 (1915–1941).
Harris, Alexandra, *Romantic Moderns* (pp.189–90, 'Virginia Woolf and Rodmell Village').
Jenkins, Simon, *England's Thousand Best Houses* (Allen Lane).
National Trust booklet, 'Virginia Woolf and Monk's House'.

AUDIO/VIDEO

A website search for 'videos of Charleston Farmhouse' provides links to several clips which chain together.
www.youtube.com/watch?v=8uw49axuvXA (3 minutes. 02 seconds: 'Charleston; A Bloomsbury House').

WEBSITES

www.bloomsburyinsussex.org.uk.
www.charleston.org.uk.
www.nationaltrust.org.uk/monks-house.

Relevant websites found by searches for 'Charleston', 'Monk's House', 'Vanessa Bell', 'Virginia Woolf', 'David Garnett', 'Bloomsbury Group', 'stream of consciousness', 'bipolar disorder', 'Charleston dance'.

5   PEVENSEY CASTLE

PRINT

Broad, Mark, 'St Crispin's Day – the Battle of Agincourt, October 25th 1415', *Magnet* magazine, October 2015 (pp.24–25).
English Heritage, 'Guidebook: Pevensey Castle'.
Mortimer, Ian, *The Fears of Henry IV* (pp.172, 287, 341, 350).
Mortimer, Ian, *1415 Henry V's Year of Glory* (pp.62, 98–99, 181, 282–83).
Pryor, Francis, *Britain AD* (pp.135–43, 'Saxon Shore Forts').

AUDIO/VIDEO

www.youtube.com/watch?v=UB402O8KYKc (4 minutes 3 seconds: A video tour of the Pevensey Castle site).

WEBSITES

www.english-heritage.org.uk/visit/places/pevensey-castle.
www.sussexarch.org.uk/saaf/pevensey.html (includes a detailed account of the archaeological investigations and Lady Joan Pelham's letter in the original Middle English).
www.sussexcastles.com/castles/pevensey-castle.html (includes a slideshow).
www.timetravel-britain.com/articles/castles/pevensey2.shtml ('The Ghosts of Pevensey Castle', a spine-tingling article by Elizabeth Wright, drawing on the ghost tales of Robert Slater, host of the Pevensey Castle Ghost Walks).

Relevant websites found by searches for 'Pevensey Castle', 'Saxon Shore', '1066 Country Walk', 'Saxon Shore Way'.

FOR WALKERS

www.ldwa.org.uk – the Long Distance Walkers Association website contains details of both the connected 1066 Country Walk and the Saxon Shore Way. The 1066 Country Walk (westwards) also connects up with the South Downs Way at Jevington. The walks take you through Pevensey Castle (on OS Explorer Map 123, labelled 'Pevensey Castle and Anderitum Roman Fort') and the 1066 battle site, among other historic sites in Sussex. OS Landranger Maps 199 and 189 cover the Sussex section. The Saxon Shore Way coastal footpath (eastwards) finishes at Gravesend in Kent.

6 THE ROYAL PAVILION, BRIGHTON

PRINT

Jenkins, Simon, *England's Thousand Best Houses* (pp.756–59).
McGough, Roger (foreword), *Poetry Please* (*Kubla Khan* by Samuel Taylor Coleridge is on p.116).
The Royal Pavilion Guide – the official guidebook, available in the on-site shop or the online shop (http://shop.brighton-hove-museums.org.uk). There are several other titles available, including a young person's guide for 7–11-year-olds, by Deborah Rooney.
Tolkien, J.R.R., *The Hobbit* (Tolkien's own illustration, *Conversation with Smaug*, faces p.224, text extract from p.227).

AUDIO/VIDEO

https://vimeo.com/25501536 (4 minutes 42 seconds: 'A dark day in Paradise. Clare Twomey at the Royal Pavilion Brighton', Arts Council England – an artist's response to the Pavilion).

www.youtube.com/watch?v=Pay6hkMOuW4 (8 minutes 55 seconds: A short history narrated by Andrew Barlow, a former keeper of the Royal Pavilion, as provided for visitors. Contains on-screen subtitles and signing. This chains on to several further clips).

WEBSITES

http://brightonmuseums.org.uk/royalpavilion (the Royal Pavilion and Museums' official website – extensive and beautifully illustrated). www.sikhmuseum.com/brighton (the history of the use of the Royal Pavilion, and two other sites, as a hospital for British Indian Army soldiers during the First World War). www.open.edu/openlearn/history-the-arts/history/history-art/brighton-pavilion/content-section-0 (extracts from a free online nine-unit, sixteen-hour course, 'Brighton Pavilion', by the Open University).

Relevant websites found by searches for 'Royal Pavilion Brighton', 'Queen Victoria's children', '*Here There Be Dragons*', '*Crouching Tiger, Hidden Dragon*'.

7   THE PRIORY OF ST PANCRAS & LEWES CASTLE

PRINT

Farmer, David Hugh, *The Oxford Dictionary of Saints* (Pancras of Rome, p.335).
Jenkins, Simon, *England's Thousand Best Houses* (Allen Lane, 'Lewes Castle', p.775).
Lee, Christopher, *This Sceptred Isle 55BC–1901* (Chapter 9, 1217–72, pp.92–97).
Lewes Pictorial Tourist Map (resortmaps.com, freely available at various outlets in the town).
Morris, Marc, *A Great and Terrible King: Edward I and the Forging of Britain* (from the Battle of Lewes to the Battle of Evesham, pp.61-69).
OS Landranger Map 198, 'Brighton & Lewes' (indicates the 1264 Battle of Lewes site, Offham Hill, NW of Lewes).
Sussex Past, Lewes Castle & Barbican House Museum (Sussex Archaeological Society).

AUDIO/VIDEO CLIPS

https://vimeo.com/107141055 (10 minutes 02 seconds: A tour of the Priory of St Pancras produced by the Lewes Priory Trust, with a particular emphasis on their work with local schools).
https://vimeo.com/41063043 (6 minutes 16 seconds: 'The Bald Explorer: The Battle of Lewes').
https://audioboom.com/boos/1080174-the-song-of-the-battle-of-lewes (1 minute 46 seconds, audio: In Middle English, the language of the time. The first four stanzas are read by Dr Carl Schmidt, Balliol College, Oxford).
www.bbc.co.uk/news/uk-england-sussex-27416317 (1 minute 50 seconds: 'Battle of Lewes Tapestry Unveiled', Mark Sanders, BBC *South-East Today*, 15 May 2014).

WEBSITES

www.bbc.co.uk/news/uk-england-27373398 ('Battle of Lewes: England's first fight for democracy?' Nick Tarver, *BBC News*, 14 May 2014).

www.british-history.ac.uk/vch/sussex/vol2/pp64-71 (British History Online – A detailed history of the Priory of Lewes, from the *Victoria County History*, 1973).

www.lewespriory.org.uk (the Lewes Priory Trust website).

www.sussexpast.co.uk/properties-to-discover/lewes-castle (the Sussex Archaeological Society website).

https://sussexpast.co.uk/battle-of-lewes-main/where-was-the-battle-of-lewes-fought.

Relevant websites found by searches for 'Priory of St Pancras', 'Lewes Castle', 'Battle of Lewes', 'Lewes Museum', 'Battle of Lewes tapestry', '*The Song of Lewes*', 'St Pancras of Rome', 'St Pancras Old Church', 'William de Warenne, 1st Earl of Surrey'.

8   THE LIBERATOR MEMORIAL

PRINT

Farmer, Ben, 'Flying Farewell', *The Daily Telegraph*, Thursday, 15 October 2015, pp.8–9 (a short feature accompanying a superb large image (Andy Rouse) of Vulcan XH558 seen flying through light cloud over Beachy Head with the lighthouse below).

McLachlan, Ian and J. Zorn Russell, *Eighth Air Force Bomber Stories* (Chapter 8, 'Hurry Home Boys').

Watson, Kevin Peter, *RUTH-LESS and Far From Home: An American B-24D Liberator Bomber at War*.

AUDIO/VIDEO

www.youtube.com/watch?v=NqEvhKgXBAE (9 minutes: The Liberator Memorial dedication in May 1995).

WEBSITES

www.44thbombgroup.com (the 44th Bomb Group Second World War database. Click on 'Roll of Honor', scroll down to page 203, July 2005 edition).

www.publicsculpturesofsussex.co.uk/object?id=65 (a description of the *Ruth-less* memorial, with photos and a history).

Relevant websites found by searches for 'Liberator Memorial Eastbourne', 'Watten, Pas-de-Calais', 'RAF Shipdham', 'Liberator aircraft', 'Liberator Memorial Eastbourne Annual Remembrance Service', 'Battle of Britain Memorial Flight', 'Canadian Lancaster Bomber', 'heavy bomber aircraft', 'Avro Vulcan bomber', 'V-bombers', 'Cold War', 'Tornado aircraft', 'Typhoon aircraft', 'Boeing 747', 'Airbourne'.

OTHER

There is a Corgi Aviation Archive Collector Series model of *Ruth-less* (an image is available by a website search for this title).

9 UPPARK HOUSE AND GARDEN

PRINT

Jenkins, Simon, *England's Thousand Best Houses* (pp.789–91).
Wells, H.G., *The Time Machine* (Heinemann text).

AUDIO/VIDEO

https://vimeo.com/album/1573545 (2 minutes 44 seconds to 10 minutes 42 seconds: A collection of five videos about the fire and restoration of Uppark).
www.youtube.com/watch?v=HcXN1PwWLug (2 minutes 59 seconds: A tour of Uppark, commissioned by the National Trust from Sheffield House).
https://youtube.com/watch?v=yYTDs77yXEI (4 minutes 08 seconds: Sarah Brightman sings 'Early One Morning').

WEBSITES

http://infobritain.co.uk/Uppark.htm (outlines the connection between Uppark and the H.G. Wells novel, *The Time Machine*).
www.nationaltrust.org.uk/uppark-house-and-garden.

Relevant websites found by searches for 'Uppark House', 'Phoenix', 'Grand Tour', 'Lady Emma Hamilton', 'HMS *Victory*', 'H.G. Wells', '*The Time Machine*'.

10 WEALD AND DOWNLAND OPEN AIR MUSEUM

PRINT

Jenkins, Simon, *England's Thousand Best Houses* (pp.784–88).
Morris, Christopher, *William Cobbett's Illustrated Rural Rides 1821–32*, Singleton (Sussex), Saturday 2 August 1823 (p.76).
Ordnance Survey, OS Landranger Map 197: Chichester & the South Downs (William Cobbett's Rural Ride can be traced, over the viewpoint, Duncton Down ('Dunton') via Upwaltham and East Dean to Singleton).
'Weald and Downland Open Air Museum' (publicity leaflet).

AUDIO/VIDEO

www.bbc.co.uk/programmes/p01s2n61 (12 minutes, audio: 'Singleton, Sussex: First WI Meeting', BBC Sussex & Surrey, *World War One at Home*, 11 February 2014).
www.youtube.com/user/wealddownlandmuseum/videos (36 seconds to 16 minutes 18 seconds: A set of videos about various aspects of and activities at the museum).

www.youtube.com/watch?v=czkaGKuvLyw (2x44minutes: *Most Haunted: Weald and Downland*, parts 1 & 2, July 2010, Living TV Channel).

WEBSITES

www.openairclassroom.org.uk (resources for teachers).
www.thewi.org.uk/about-the-wi/history-of-the-wi/the-origins.
www.wealddown.co.uk (The museum's own extensive website with excellent photos).

Relevant websites found by searches for 'Weald and Downland Open Air Museum', 'quotes about old houses', 'Piers Plowman', 'Saint Swithin', 'Weald and Downland Museum Most Haunted'.

II PETWORTH HOUSE AND PARK

PRINT

Rose, Rebecca, 'Turner at Petworth', *Financial Times*, 10 October 2009.
The Tate Gallery, *The Turner Collection in the Clore Gallery* (pp.65–73, Room 102, Petworth and East Cowes).
Riding, Jacqueline & Andrew Loukes, *Mr. Turner: An Exhibition* (National Trust, produced to accompany an exhibition at Petworth House, 10 January– 11 March 2015, inspired by Mike Leigh's film *Mr Turner*, Thin Man Films).
Bailey, Anthony, *John Constable: A Kingdom of his Own* (pp.257–60).
Chaucer, Geoffrey, 'The Cook's Prologue and Tale', *The Canterbury Tales*.
Wintle, Angela, 'At Home with Lord Egremont at Petworth House', *Sussex Life*, 25 May 2011 (Lord Egremont, aka Max Egremont, acclaimed novelist and biographer, talks of life at Petworth and of his writing career).

AUDIO/VIDEO

www.youtube.com/watch?v=cRzePD46voA (2 minutes 13 seconds: A video tour of Petworth House and park produced for the National Trust. This site also provides access to other clips).

WEBSITES

www.nationaltrust.org.uk/petworth-house.

Relevant websites found by searches for 'Petworth House', 'Turner at Petworth', 'Hans Holbein the Younger', 'Egremont'.

12 CHICHESTER CATHEDRAL

PRINT

Broad, Mark, 'Thomas Weelkes' (Sussex History), *Magnet* magazine, November 2015, pp.24–25.

Farmer, David Hugh, *The Oxford Dictionary of Saints* ('Martha', pp.286–87;
'Richard of Chichester', pp.369–70).
The New English Bible.
'Welcome – Chichester Cathedral', visitor leaflet (includes a floorplan and brief
descriptions of all the artefacts and areas of particular interest).

AUDIO/VIDEO

www.goldmarkart.com/scholarship/john-piper-chichester-cathedral
(2 minutes 35 seconds: John Piper's 'Chichester Cathedral' tapestry).
www.youtube.com/watch?v=acXxM2WAeNE (3 minutes 07 seconds: Philip
Larkin reads his poem *An Arundel Tomb*).
www.youtube.com/watch?v=S0POv7HrjRc (9 minutes 03 seconds: Andrew
Graham Dixon discusses the important Lambert Barnard paintings in the
cathedral, a *Culture Show Special*, 2010).

WEBSITES

www.chichestercathedral.org.uk (the official website – excellent). www.
chichestercathedral.org.uk/dyn/_assets/_pdfs/StRichardofChichester.pdf
(a short biography of St Richard).
www.leonardbernstein.com/works_chichester_psalms.htm (a full account of
the music's development).

Relevant websites found by searches for 'Chichester Cathedral Art', 'Paintings
of Chichester Cathedral', 'Philip Larkin's poem *An Arundel Tomb*, 'Quotes about
Chichester Cathedral', 'Collapse of Chichester Cathedral Spire', 'St Richard
of Chichester'.

13 ARUNDEL CASTLE

PRINT

Jenkins, Simon, *England's Thousand Best Houses* (pp.746–49).
Taylor, Andrew, *The Pocket Guide to Poets & Poetry* (Henry Howard, p.24).

AUDIO/VIDEO

A website search for 'videos of Arundel Castle' provides links to several clips.

WEBSITES

www.arundel.org.uk/local-info/arundel-facts (contains an extract from Queen
Victoria's journal entry about her visit).
www.arundelcastle.org (Arundel Castle official website).
www.castles.org/dokuwiki/castlesoftheworld/england/arundel (includes a
section on the ghosts and a comprehensive family history).
http://historytodaymagazine.blogspot.com/2009/03/not-so-secret-diary-
of-queen-victoria.html (extracts from Queen Victoria's journal describing her

three-day visit to Arundel Castle with Prince Albert, 1–3 December 1846).

Relevant websites found by searches for 'Arundel Castle', 'Arundel Castle Cricket Club', 'Queen Victoria's visit to Arundel Castle'.

14 NYMAN'S

PRINT

Jenkins, Simon, *England's Thousand Best Houses* (pp.776–77).
Grahame, Kenneth, *The Wind in the Willows* (illustrated in colour by Ernest H. Shepard). (Illustration of Toad Hall showing giant Monkey Puzzle tree, p.226).
National Trust, 'Welcome to Nyman's in Summer' (visitors' pamphlet).
Sussex Life, October 2013 (pp.195–96).

AUDIO/VIDEO

www.bbc.co.uk/programmes/p01xs59w (2 minutes 35 seconds: from the BBC4 programme on Nyman's – episode 4 of 4 of their series *British Gardens in Time*, 2014 – Chris Beardshaw presents).

WEBSITES

www.nationaltrust.org.uk/nymans.

Relevant websites found by searches for 'Nyman's house and garden', 'Monkey Puzzle tree at Nyman's', 'Anthony Armstrong-Jones'.

15 FISHBOURNE ROMAN PALACE AND GARDENS & BIGNOR ROMAN VILLA

PRINT

Jenkins, Simon, *England's Thousand Best Houses* (Fishbourne Roman Palace, p.766).
'Fishbourne Roman Palace & Gardens' (site map).
Pryor, Francis, *Britain AD* (pp.101, 116–17).
Scullard, H.H., *Roman Britain: Outpost of the Empire* (pp.50, 119, 122).
Ordnance Survey, 'Map of Roman Britain' (3rd. Edition), Scale 16 miles to One Inch.
Robb, Graham, *The Ancient Paths* (pp.242–43).
McGough, Roger (foreword), 'The Roman Centurion's Song', *Poetry Please* (pp.446–47).

AUDIO/VIDEO

Relevant websites found by searches for:
'Videos of Fishbourne Roman Palace' (brings up links to several YouTube videos, from 2 minutes 20 seconds – with an appearance by the Ermine Street Guard Roman Army Re-enactment Society; up to one of 16 minutes 30 seconds).
'Videos of Bignor Roman Villa' (brings up a link to a short YouTube video (1 minute) and one of 7 minutes).

'Videos of the Roman Occupation of Britain' (brings up a three-part series of 45 minute programmes *The Roman Invasion of Britain* with Bettany Hughes (the Smithsonian Channel) on YouTube).

WEBSITES

www.bignorromanvilla.co.uk (the official site).
www.sussexpast.co.uk/properties-to-discover/fishbourne-roman-palace (the excellent Sussex Archaeological Society official site).

Relevant websites found by searches for '*Veni, Vidi, Vici*', 'Fishbourne Roman Palace', 'Bignor Roman Villa'.

16 STANDEN HOUSE AND GARDEN

PRINT

Jenkins, Simon, *England's Thousand Best Houses* (p.788).
MacCarthy, Fiona, *William Morris: A Life for Our Time*.
National Trust, 'Welcome to Standen' (visitors leaflet, including map).
Russell, Beth, *Victorian Needlepoint* – a book for needle workers containing Arts and Crafts designs to work. Those found at Standen are 'Strawberry Thief I' (pp.14–18) and 'Acanthus' (pp.68–73).
Taylor, Andrew, *The Pocket Guide to Poets and Poetry* (William Morris is on pp.68–69).

AUDIO/VIDEO

https://vimeo.com/album/3438607/video/139830081 (11 minutes 36 seconds: Part 1 of a 3-part series on the History of the Arts and Crafts Movement, with superb images).
www.youtube.com/watch?v=NInLOkXmAMs (2 minutes 29 seconds: A video tour of Standen House and garden produced for the National Trust. This site also provides access to other clips).

WEBSITES

www.nationaltrust.org.uk/standen-house-and-garden.
www.periodproperty.co.uk/ppuk_discovering_ppom_201004.shtml (an enjoyable account of the history and family life of Standen, published as an article in a series 'Period Property of the Month', April 2010).
www.william-morris.co.uk/a-full-history (This is the website of the original Morris & Co., still a thriving business today).

Relevant websites found by searches for 'Standen House and garden', 'Philip Webb', 'Arts and Crafts Movement', 'Morris & Co.', 'William De Morgan', 'The Beale family of Standen', 'Standen Garden Revival', 'The Sussex Chair', 'The Red House Bexleyheath'.

17 ERIC RAVILIOUS

PRINT

Constable, Freda, with Sue Simon, *The England of Eric Ravilious* (includes a
    biography).
Laity, Paul, 'Ups and Downs', *Saturday Guardian Review*, 30 April 2011.
MacFarlane, Robert, *The Old Ways* (an account of Ravilious' time in the Arctic
    Circle, pp.299–302).
Powers, Alan, *Eric Ravilious: Imagined Realities*.
Russell, James, *Ravilious in Pictures: Sussex and the Downs* (each watercolour
    reproduced is accompanied by a short essay).
Russell, James, *Ravilious in Pictures: The War Paintings*.
Russell, James, *Ravilious: The Watercolours*.

AUDIO/VIDEO

Relevant websites found by searches for 'videos about Eric Ravilious' include:
    An exhibition preview of Ravilious at Dulwich Picture Gallery, April–
August 2015 (2 minutes 42 seconds).
    Frank Muir commenting on Eric Ravilious' *Runway Perspective* (1942) (1
minute 15 secs).
    Raymond Briggs commenting on Eric Ravilious' *Thrice Welcome* (1935)
wood engravings (1 min 11 seconds).

WEBSITES

www.publicdomainreview.org/2013/11/27/time-and-place-eric-ravilious-1903-1942
(a particularly interesting article on Ravilious by Frank Delaney).

Relevant websites found by searches for 'Eric Ravilious', 'portrait of Eric
Ravilious', 'Eric Ravilious watercolours'.

A PLACE TO VISIT

Towner Gallery, Eastbourne, holds one of the largest public collections of
Ravilious' work. The dedicated 'Ravilious Room', supported by Eastbourne
Arts Circle, contains a selection of his finest works, including watercolours,
sketches and woodcuts. There are also items from the Ravilious archive,
including a wide range of Ravilious books. The display is regularly refreshed.
Further works from the complete collection can be viewed during the regular
hour-long guided art store tours.

18 ALAN TURING

PRINT

There are very many books and articles relating to Alan Turing. A couple of the
more unusual ones are:

Davies, Caroline, 'Codebreaker Turing is Given Posthumous Royal Pardon',
 Guardian (front page, 24 December 2013).
'My Hero', *Guardian* article series, the choice of the writer Alan Garner (2011).
Stephenson, Neal, *Cryptonomicon*.

AUDIO/VIDEO

www.bbc.co.uk/history/places/bletchley_park (contains six video clip
highlights of relevant BBC TV programmes).
The Imitation Game (Black Bear Pictures, 2014).
www.telegraph.co.uk/history/world-war-two/10536246/Alan-Turing-
granted-Royal-pardon-by-the-Queen.html (1 minute 27 seconds: 'Turing
"a war hero like Churchill"', Chris Grayling, the Justice Secretary, speaking on
the occasion of the granting of Turing's royal pardon).

WEBSITES

Relevant websites found by searches for 'Alan Turing', 'Bletchley Park', 'GCHQ',
'computer games', 'world wide web', 'poison victims', 'Apple company logo', 'early
computer developments', 'artificial intelligence', 'Turing Test', 'Turing Award',
'Alan Turing pardon', 'quotes by Alan Turing', '*Imitation Game*'.

19 SIR ARTHUR CONAN DOYLE

PRINT

Doyle, Sir Arthur Conan, *The Lost World* (Professor Challenger).
Doyle, Sir Arthur Conan, *A Study in Scarlet, The Final Problem, The Hound of the
 Baskervilles, The Adventure of the Empty House, His Last Bow* (Sherlock Holmes).
King, Susan, 'Elementary, Dear Watson!', *Eastbourne Herald*, 13 June 2014
 (review of James Lovegrove's second Sherlock Holmes novel, *Gods of War*,
 set in the countryside between Eastbourne and the Cuckmere Valley).

AUDIO/VIDEO

www.youtube.com/watch?v=4eq18U5btcg (10 minutes, monochrome:
'Sir Arthur Conan Doyle, creator of Sherlock Holmes' rare interview).
Also, a large number of video clips can be found by website searches for 'video
clips of Sherlock Holmes'. Sherlock Holmes is listed as 'most portrayed movie
character' in *Guinness World Records* (over seventy actors in over 200 films).

WEBSITES

www.cbgc.co.uk/press (the website of Crowborough Beacon Golf Club. Click
on 'Sir Arthur Conan Doyle – *Great Golf Magazine* – May 2013'. An article
which includes an account of Doyle's connection with the club).
http://en.wikipedia.org/wiki/Sherlock_Holmes (an extensive biography of the
fictional detective).

www.nanowrimo.org (the website for the National Novel Writing Month).
www.sherlockholmesonline.org (the official website of the Sir Arthur Conan Doyle Literary Estate).

Relevant websites found by searches for 'Sir Arthur Conan Doyle', 'Sherlock Holmes', 'Sherlock Holmes blue plaque in East Dean', 'Sherlock Holmes retirement cottage'.

DERIVED WORKS

There are hundreds of 'derived' works – stories, novels, radio and television series, stage plays, films and even video games. On television, Benedict Cumberbatch plays a modern-day version of the detective, with Martin Freeman as Watson in the popular BBC1 series *Sherlock*.

20 JOHN LOGIE BAIRD

PRINT

Baird, John Logie, *Television and Me: The Memoirs of John Logie Baird*.
Kamm, Anthony and Malcom Baird, *John Logie Baird: A Life* (National Museum of Scotland Publishing).

AUDIO/VIDEO

JLB – the Man who saw the Future (2002) – seventy-four minute television documentary. This was last broadcast on BBC4 on Monday, 2 November 2009. The documentary is based on the 2002 book *John Logie Baird: A Life*. The programme is not currently available on the BBC iPlayer. However, the film footage is available in the Archive Collection, held and administered by the Alexandra Palace Television Society. The film can presently be accessed by clicking on the video link at the foot of the webpage (www.electricscotland.com/history/other/john_logie_baird.htm).

An interesting selection of short video clips can be found by searching for 'videos on John Logie Baird'.

WEBSITES

www.1066.net/baird (an illustrated article 'John Logie Baird in Hastings').
www.bairdtelevision.com – an extensive, authoritative website, updated every few months by Iain L. Baird (grandson) and Malcolm H.I. Baird (son).
www.openplaques.org/people/304 (contains images and locations of five commemorative plaques).

Relevant websites found by searches for 'John Logie Baird', 'John Logie Baird in Hastings', 'John Logie Baird in Bexhill', 'John Logie Baird television patents', 'John Logie Baird and the Flying Spot technique', 'The Crystal Palace', 'Cause of the fire at Crystal Palace', 'Lord Reith of the BBC'.

21 PERCY BYSSHE SHELLEY

PRINT

Fuller, John, *Who is Ozymandias? And Other Puzzles in Poetry* (pp.197–202).

Sampson, Ana, *I Wandered Lonely as a Cloud ... and Other Poems you Half-remember from School* (pp.59–61).

Wain, John (ed.), *The Oxford Library of English Poetry* (pp.422–57, eleven selected poems by Shelley).

Wright, David (ed.), *The Penguin Book of English Romantic Verse.*

AUDIO/VIDEO

A website search for 'videos of Percy Bysshe Shelley' provides links to several readings. A good site is that entitled 'Percy Bysshe Shelley – Ozymandias – Video Dailymotion' (a selection of celebrity readings with visuals and commentaries, also links to other Shelley poems from Poetictouch).

WEBSITES

www.burrows.co.uk/horshamguide/13Per.htm (containing some local information and a transcript of the inscription on the wall of the Field Place bedroom in which he was born).

https://en.wikipedia.org/wiki/Percy_Bysshe_Shelley.

www.poetryfoundation.org/bio/percy-bysshe-shelley.

www.who2.com/bio/percy-bysshe-shelley (with useful links to other sources).

Relevant websites found by searches for 'Percy Bysshe Shelley', 'Mary Shelley – *Frankenstein*', 'Percy Bysshe Shelley links with Sussex', 'Percy Bysshe Shelley – grave and memorials', 'Isadora Duncan'.

22 THOMAS PAINE

PRINT

'A Brief History of St Michael-in-Lewes' – this booklet is available in the church. (This is the church, across the High Street from Bull House, in which Thomas Paine was married to his second wife Elizabeth Olive – this is recorded in the marriage register for 1771. Paine also attended vestry meetings at St Michael's.)

Brent, Colin, Deborah Gage & Paul Myles, *Thomas Paine in Lewes 1768–1774. A Prelude to American Independence.*

Broad, Mark, 'Plain Truth & Common Sense – The Influential Writings of Thomas Paine', *Magnet* magazine, November 2013, pp.20–21.

'Tom Paine at Bull House' – this is a handout distributed during pre-booked weekend tours of the house.

AUDIO/VIDEO

www.bbc.co.uk/news/uk-politics-25141898 (4 minutes 49 seconds: 'Author Thomas Paine Praised by Lewes MP Norman Baker').

www.thomaspaineuk.com/Lewes.html – the UK Thomas Paine Society website, with many links, including a talk (3x21 minutes) by Dr Colin Brent at the 2009 Lewes Festival in July 2009 to celebrate the 200th anniversary of Thomas Paine's death.

www.youtube.com/watch?v=qd2AHZ22SJ8 (The song 'Tom Paine's Bones'. Words and music by Graham Moore, sung by the Scottish musician Dick Gaughan, from his album *Outlaws and Dreamers*). The lyric can be found at www.dickgaughan.co.uk/songs/texts/tpbones.html.

WEBSITES

http://articles.latimes.com/2001/apr/01/news/mn-45431 (article, 'Thomas Paine's Remains are still a Bone of Contention').

http://news.bbc.co.uk/1/hi/magazine/8089115.stm (an article by Brendan O'Neill, 'Who was Thomas Paine?').

www.britishlistedbuildings.co.uk/en-293163-bull-house-lewes-east-sussex/ photos (photos in which the plaque to Thomas Paine and 'The Satyr' carved figure by an unknown medieval craftsman can be seen).

https://sussexpast.co.uk/properties-to-discover/bull-house (contains a link to an extensive archaeological survey of the house).

www.tompaineprintingpress.com (a working eighteenth-century style wooden 'Common Press', set up by Peter Chasseaud in 2009 in Lewes. Chasseaud is a member of the revived Headstrong Club. The site has useful links to Thomas Paine information).

Relevant websites found by searches for 'Thomas Paine', 'Thomas Paine and Lewes', 'Bull House, Lewes', 'Rights of Man', 'Common Sense', 'The Age of Reason', 'Headstrong Club, Lewes', 'Thomas Paine quotes', 'UK Thomas Paine Society', 'Gettysburg Address', 'Tom Paine's bones'.

23 SIR ERNEST SHACKLETON

PRINT

McGough, Roger (foreword), *Poetry Please* (selected Browning, Keats and *If*, by Rudyard Kipling).

Shackleton, Sir Ernest, *South: The Endurance Expedition*.

Smith, Michael, *Shackleton – By Endurance We Conquer.*

AUDIO/VIDEO

A website search for 'videos of Sir Ernest Shackleton' provides links to several clips from 1 minute 26 seconds (a crew photo 'animation') to 1 hour 37 minutes 52 seconds. The latter is listed on the website 'Popular Videos – Sir Ernest Shackleton – YouTube' and is a full documentary on the Endurance Expedition.

WEBSITES

www.jamescairdsociety.com – the society, established in 1994, is dedicated to keeping the memory of Sir Ernest Shackleton alive, named after the open boat in which Shackleton and five companions made their epic 800-mile journey. A very extensive website.

www.antarctic-circle.org/llag.shackleton.htm#037 ('llag' stands for *Low Latitude Antarctic Gazetteer*, again very extensive, page 59 includes a facsimile of Shackleton's plan for the South Pole expedition which he sketched on Grand Hotel, Eastbourne, headed notepaper).

www.south-pole.com/p0000097.htm (contains detailed accounts of the expeditions).

www.openplaques.org/plaques/1185 (a blue plaque to Sir Ernest Shackleton is at 14 Milnthorpe Road, Eastbourne).

Relevant websites found by searches for 'Sir Ernest Shackleton', 'Ernest Shackleton Quotes', 'Eastbourne Blue Plaques', 'Endurance centenary events', 'Shackleton crater on the moon'.

24 WILLIAM BLAKE

PRINT

Ackroyd, Peter, *Blake*.
Blake, William, *The Complete Poems*.
Blake, William, *Selected Poems*.
Bronowski, J. (ed.), *William Blake*.
Reeves, Marjorie and Jenyth Worsley, *Favourite Hymns* (title page –
    Blake quote; pp.136–39. An interesting background note, including an
    example illuminated poem and the text of the hymn 'Jerusalem').
Sampson, Ana, *I Wandered Lonely as a Cloud* ... (pp.43–45).
Tagholm, Roger, *Walking Literary London* (pp.28, 82, Plate 18 – tombstone).

AUDIO VIDEO

Searching for 'William Blake quotes' finds a selection of video clips including an excellent must-see *South Bank Show* dramatised documentary (LWT for ITV, 52 mins). The programme starts with a sequence at the cottage in Felpham, Sussex.

www.tate.org.uk/learn/online-resources/william-blake (contains audio recordings of his poems accompanied by Blake's original handwritten illustrated texts).
www.youtube.com/watch?v=deLc8EgbOJs (2 minutes 24 seconds: a performance of the hymn 'Jerusalem' from York Minster).

WEBSITES

www.beatdom.com/william-blake-and-the-beat-generation – a short article on the influence of William Blake on the Beat Generation of poets and writers in the 1950s, particularly Allen Ginsberg (1926–97). This is one example of

Blake's continuing influence, right up to the present day, for example on the
writer Philip Pullman (*His Dark Materials*).
www.blakesociety.org/blakecottage (an article on the successful appeal which
has enabled Blake's Cottage in Felpham to be bought in trust for the nation).
www.theguardian.com/culture/2014/nov/21/the-10-best-works-by-
william-blake (on the eve of a major exhibition at the Ashmolean, Oxford,
4 December 2014–1 March 2015, Fiona Maddocks chose her ten favourite
works. No. 6 is Blake's Cottage at Felpham – with an angel descending).
www.tate.org.uk/learn/online-resources/william-blake (a brilliant website
covering most aspects of William Blake's life and work).
www.westminster-abbey.org/our-history/people/william-blake
(brief biographical details with a photo of Blake's bronze bust, by the
sculptor Sir Jacob Epstein, in Poets Corner in Westminster Abbey).

Relevant websites found by searches for 'William Blake', 'Jerusalem hymn',
'*The Tyger*, William Blake', 'William Blake quotes', 'William Blake art', 'William
Blake poems', 'William Blake books', 'Felpham, Sussex', 'William Hayley, poet',
'Romanticism', 'influences on William Blake's art', 'William Blake in popular culture'.

25 ISAMBARD KINGDOM BRUNEL

PRINT

Brunel, Isambard B.C.L., *The Life of Isambard Kingdom Brunel, Civil Engineer*
    (a comprehensive biography by his son. It has been made 'free to share' as
    an eBook by Project Gutenberg at www.gutenberg.org/files/41210/41210-
    h/41210-h.htm).
Buchanan, R. Angus, *Brunel: The Life and Times of Isambard Kingdom Brunel*.

AUDIO/VIDEO

A website search for 'videos of Isambard Kingdom Brunel' provides links to
several clips which chain together.
www.youtube.com/watch?v=FdOrpAtlt7M (3 minutes 08 seconds: 'The Life of
Isambard Kingdom Brunel' could be a starting point).
www.youtube.com/watch?v=QwHnVH9jWmU (57 minutes 42 seconds: *Great
Britons: Isambard Kingdom Brunel*, hosted by Jeremy Clarkson, BBC4 Documentary).

WEBSITES

www.history.co.uk/biographies/isambard-kingdom-brunel.
www.cliftonbridge.org.uk.
www.ssgreatbritain.org.

Relevant websites found by searches for 'Isambard Kingdom Brunel',
'Dr Morrell's Boarding School, Hove', 'origin of the name Isambard', 'Breguet
clocks and watches', 'Clifton Suspension Bridge', 'NHS foundation by Aneurin

Bevan', 'Swindon railway village birthplace of the NHS', 'Box Tunnel Brunel', 'Thames Tunnel Brunel', 'Isambard Kingdom Brunel quotes'.

26 SIR PATRICK MOORE

PRINT

Moore, Patrick, *Patrick Moore: The Autobiography* (the original version was published under the title *80 not out: The Autobiography*, 2003).

AUDIO/VIDEO

www.youtube.com/watch?v=6t0exJznEZg (20 minutes: Sir Patrick Moore's final episode of *The Sky at Night – Reaching for the Stars*, 6 January 2013. This was mostly filmed in the garden of his house in Selsey, 'within the sound of the sea'). YouTube then continues on to the 2-hour BBC 2008 *Sky at Night* Moon special 'Apollo: A Night to Remember'. Sir Patrick was one of the presenters. The night was 16 July 1969, the launch of Apollo 11, the first manned flight to the moon. The programme is prefaced by an extract from President Kennedy's historic 25 May 1961 speech committing the USA to sending a man to the moon. www.youtube.com/watch?v=8ZF4qyOPrcU (3 minutes 11 seconds: *The Sky at Night* theme tune, the first movement from 'Pélleas et Mélisande: At the Castle Gate' by Jean Sibelius).

WEBSITES

http://banguniverse.com (an interactive website set up by Brian May, Patrick Moore and Chris Lintott to stimulate constructive discussion of the astronomical topics raised in their jointly authored books, *Bang! The Complete History of the Universe* (2006), and *The Cosmic Tourist* (2012). The website also has a link to the Sir Patrick Moore Memorial website containing many moving personal tributes to Sir Patrick as well as 'Latest News' features).
www.bbc.co.uk/news/uk-20657939 ('Sir Patrick Moore, astronomer and broadcaster, dies aged 89', posted 9 December 2012. This also has three video clips embedded).
www.dailymail.co.uk/news/article-2245616 (a particularly enjoyable obituary by Glenys Roberts).
www.brianmay.com/brian/brianssb/brianssboct15a.html#07 ('Patrick Moore Legacy', Friday, 9 October 2015, Brian May's plans for Sir Patrick's estate. May was a close friend of Sir Patrick and one of the executors of his will).

Relevant websites found by searches for 'Sir Patrick Moore', 'Ptolemy', 'Farthings, Selsey', 'Sir Patrick Moore quotes', 'Sir Patrick Moore obituaries', 'Sir Patrick Moore GamesMaster', 'Sir Patrick Moore xylophone', 'Brian May and the Sky at Night', 'The Master of the Moon by Patrick Moore', 'At the Castle Gate'.

BIBLIOGRAPHY

Arscott, David, *The Little Book of Sussex* (The History Press: Stroud, Gloucestershire, 2011).

ArtFund, *Art Fund Guide 2015* (National Art Collections Fund: Melksham, Wiltshire 2015).

Bailey, Anthony, *John Constable: A Kingdom of his Own* (Vintage Books: London, 2007).

Baird, John Logie, *Television and Me: The Memoirs of John Logie Baird* (Mercat Press: Edinburgh, 2004).

Batsford, Harry and Charles Fry, *The English Cottage* (3rd Edition, Batsford Books, The 'British Heritage' Series: London, 1950).

Bell, Anne Olivier (ed.), *The Diary of Virginia Woolf*, Volumes 1 to 5 (Penguin Books: Harmondsworth, 1979–85).

Blake, William, *The Complete Poems* (Penguin Classics, 2004).

Blake, William, *Selected Poems* (Penguin Classics, 2006).

Brandon, Peter, *The Discovery of Sussex* (Phillimore & Co. Ltd: Andover, Hampshire, 2010).

Brent, Colin, Deborah Gage and Paul Myles, *Thomas Paine in Lewes 1768–1774. A Prelude to American Independence* (Pm Press: Oakland, California, 2009).

Brickell, Christopher (ed.), *The Royal Horticultural Society New Encyclopaedia of Plants and Flowers* (Dorling Kindersley: London, 1999).

Bronowski, J. (ed.), *William Blake* (Penguin Books, 'The Penguin Poets' Series: Harmondsworth, 1958).

Buchanan, R. Angus, *Brunel: The Life and Times of Isambard Kingdom Brunel* (A&C Black: London, 2006).

Butler, Adam, Claire Van Cleave and Susan Stirling, *The Art Book* (Phaidon Press Ltd: London, 1994).

Carey, John, *What Good are the Arts?* (Faber and Faber, London, 2005).

Chaucer, Geoffrey, 'The Cook's Prologue and Tale' in *Canterbury Tales* (various editions available).

Clarke, Stephen, *1,000 Years of Annoying the French* (Black Swan: London, 2011).

Constable, Freda, with Sue Simon, *The England of Eric Ravilious* (Scolar Press: London, 1983).

Craig, W.J. (ed.), *A Midsummer Night's Dream*, in *The Complete Works of William Shakespeare* (Oxford University Press: London, 1962).

Dell, Marion and Marion Whybrow, *Virginia Woolf & Vanessa Bell: Remembering St Ives* (Tabb House: Padstow, Cornwall, 2004).

Dickens, Charles, *A Tale of Two Cities* (The Oxford Illustrated Dickens, Oxford University Press: Oxford, 1978).

Doyle, Sir Arthur Conan, *The Lost World* (Professor Challenger novels: various editions available).

Doyle, Sir Arthur Conan, *A Study in Scarlet, The Final Problem, The Hound of the Baskervilles, The Adventure of the Empty House, His Last Bow* (Sherlock Holmes stories and novels: various editions available).

Duffy, Eamon, *The Stripping of the Altars* (Yale University Press: New Haven and London, 1992).

Farmer, David Hugh, *The Oxford Dictionary of Saints* (Oxford University Press: Oxford, 1987).

Fuller, John, *Who is Ozymandias? And Other Puzzles in Poetry* (Vintage Books: London, 2013).

Gardner, Helen, *Art through the Ages* (4th Edition, G. Bell and Sons Ltd: London, 1959).

Grahame, Kenneth (illustrated in colour by Ernest H. Shepard), *The Wind in the Willows* (Methuen Children's Books: London, 1971).

Harris, Alexandra, *Romantic Moderns* (Thames & Hudson, 2010).

Jenkins, Simon, *England's Thousand Best Houses* (Allen Lane: London, 2003).

Jones, Griff Rhys (foreword), 'If', 'The Glory of the Garden', 'Ozymandias', and 'Love's Philosophy' in *The Nation's Favourite Poems* (BBC: London, 1996).

Kipling, Rudyard, *The Jungle Book*, (the original edition was published in 1894, followed by *The Second Jungle Book* in 1895, various editions are currently available).

Lee, Christopher, *This Sceptred Isle 55BC–1900* (Penguin Books/BBC Books: London, 1998).

Lovegrove, James, *Sherlock Holmes: Gods of War* (Titan Books: London, 2014).

MacCarthy, Fiona, *William Morris: A Life for Our Time* (Faber & Faber: London, 1994).

MacFarlane, Robert, *The Old Ways* (Penguin Books: London, 2013).

McGough, Roger (foreword), *Poetry Please* (Faber and Faber: London, 2013).

McLachlan, Ian and Russel J. Zorn, 'Hurry Home Boys', *Eighth Air Force Bomber Stories*, Chapter 8 (Patrick Stephens Ltd: London, 1991).

Moore, Sir Patrick, *Patrick Moore: The Autobiography* (The History Press: Stroud, Gloucestershire, 2005).

Morris, Christopher, *Selections from William Cobbett's Illustrated Rural Rides 1821–32* (Webb & Bower Pubs Ltd: Exeter, Devon, 1992).

Morris, Marc, *A Great and Terrible King: Edward I and the Forging of Britain* (Windmill Books: London, 2009).

Mortimer, Ian, *1415 Henry V's Year of Glory* (Vintage Books: London, 2010).

Mortimer, Ian, *The Fears of Henry IV* (Vintage Books: London, 2008).

Mortimer, Ian, *The Time Traveller's Guide to Elizabethan England* (Vintage: London, 2013).

National Trust, *National Trust Handbook 2015* (National Trust: London, 2015).

The New English Bible (Oxford University Press & Cambridge University Press: Oxford, 1970).

Parker, Mike, *Mapping the Roads* (AA Publishing: Basingstoke, 2013).

Powers, Alan, *Eric Ravilious: Imagined Realities* (Philip Wilson Publishers Ltd: London, 2012).

Pryor, Francis, *Britain AD* (Harper Perennial: London, 2005).

Reeves, Marjorie and Worsley, Jenyth, *Favourite Hymns: 2000 Years of Magnificat* (Continuum: London, 2001).

Riding, Jacqueline and Andrew Loukes, *Mr. Turner: An Exhibition* (National Trust: Swindon, Wiltshire, 2015).

Robb, Graham, *The Ancient Paths* (Picador: London, 2014).

Russell, Beth, 'Strawberry Thief I' and 'Acanthus' in *Victorian Needlepoint* (Anaya Publishers Ltd: London, 1989).

Russell, James, *Ravilious in Pictures: Sussex and the Downs* (The Mainstone Press: Norwich, 2009).

Russell, James, *Ravilious in Pictures: The War Paintings* (The Mainstone Press: Norwich, 2010).

Russell, James, *Ravilious: The Watercolours* (Philip Wilson Publishers Ltd: London, 2015).

Sampson, Ana, *I Wandered Lonely as a Cloud …* (Michael O'Mara Books Ltd: London, 2013).

Savage, Anne (tr.), *The Anglo-Saxon Chronicles* (Illustrated edition, Phoebe Phillips/ Heinemann: London, 1982).

Scullard, H.H., *Roman Britain: Outpost of the Empire* (Thames and Hudson: London, 1999).

Shackleton, Sir Ernest, *South: The Endurance Expedition* (Penguin Modern Classics 183: Harmondsworth, 2015).

Smith, Michael, *Shackleton – By Endurance We Conquer* (The Collins Press: Wilton, Cork 2014).

Stephenson, Neal, *Cryptonomicon* (Arrow: London, 2000).

Tagholm, Roger, *Walking Literary London* (New Holland: London, 2001).

Tate Gallery, *The Turner Collection in the Clore Gallery* (Tate Gallery Publications: London, 1987).

Taylor, Andrew, *The Pocket Guide to Poets & Poetry* (Remember When: Barnsley, south Yorkshire, 2011).

The Times Concise Atlas of the World (Times Books for The Book People Ltd: London, 2008).

Tolkien, J.R.R., *The Hobbit* (3rd HB Edition, George Allen & Unwin Ltd: London, 1966).

Trautmann Banks, Joanne (ed.), *Vintage Woolf: Selected Letters* (Vintage Books: London, 2008).

Wain, John (ed.), *The Oxford Library of English Poetry* (3 vols) (BCA by arrangement with Oxford University Press: London, 1993).

Watson, Kevin Peter, *RUTH-LESS and Far From Home: An American B-24D Liberator Bomber at War* (Privately printed PB: Eastbourne, Sussex, 2000).

Wells, H.G., *The Time Machine*, (Heinemann text version, first published 1895 – various editions available).

Wheeler, Sir Mortimer, *Roman Art and Architecture* (Thames and Hudson: London, 1976).

Wood, Michael, *In Search of England* (Penguin Books: London, 2000).

Wood, Michael, *The Story of England* (Penguin Books: London, 2011).

Wright, David (ed.), *The Penguin Book of English Romantic Verse* (Penguin Books: Harmondsworth, 1968).

ORDNANCE SURVEY MAPS

OS Explorer Map 123: Eastbourne & Beachy Head.

OS Landranger Map 197: Chichester & the South Downs.

OS Landranger Map 198: Brighton & Lewes.

OS Landranger Map 199: Eastbourne & Hastings.

Ordnance Survey, Map of Roman Britain (3rd Edition), Scale: 16 miles to 1 inch (Ordnance Survey: Southampton, 1956).

Printed by Amazon Italia Logistica S.r.l.
Torrazza Piemonte (TO), Italy

16373824R00112